The Reflecting Glass

THE REFLECTING GLASS

Professional Coaching for Leadership Development

Lucy West

and

Mike Milan

palgrave

First published 2001 by
PALGRAVE
Houndmills, Basingstoke, Hampshire RG21 6XS and
175 Fifth Avenue, New York, N.Y. 10010
Companies and representatives throughout the world

PALGRAVE is the new global academic imprint of
St. Martin's Press LLC Scholarly and Reference Division and
Palgrave Publishers Ltd (formerly Macmillan Press Ltd).

ISBN-13: 978-9-333 -94529-2 hardback
ISBN-10: 0-333-94529-8   hardback

This book is printed on paper suitable for recycling and
made from fully managed and sustained forest sources.

A catalogue record for this book is available
from the British Library.

Library of Congress Cataloging-in-Publication Data

West, Lucy.
  The reflecting glass : professional coaching for leadership
development / Lucy West.
    p. cm.
  Includes bibliographical references and index.
  ISBN 0–333–94529–8
   1. Executives—Training of. 2. Leadership—Study and
teaching. 3. Mentoring in business. 4. Business consultants.
I. Title.

HD30.4 . W47 2001
658.4'07124—dc21
                                    2001036024
Editing and origination by
Aardvark Editorial, Mendham, Suffolk

10 9 8 7 6 5 4 3 2
10 9 08 07 06 05

Printed and bound in Great Britain by
Creative Print & Design (Wales), Ebbw Vale

CONTENTS

Contents

List of Figures and Tables

Figures

Tables

Lucy West graduated with honours from Georgetown University in Washington DC, and moved to London as a public relations consultant with Edelman Public Relations. She worked primarily in the health care sector, developing and implementing campaigns to promote pharmaceutical products (for which she won an industry award).

She subsequently obtained an MBA (with distinction) from London Business School before joining Andersen Consulting's (now Accenture's) change management practice. At Andersen, Lucy specialised in organisation design and development, and especially post-merger integration, across a range of industries (including telecommunications, banking, utilities and insurance).

In 1997, she joined GHN (now Penna Executive Coaching), at the time the UK's leading dedicated coaching company. While at GHN, she coached senior executives across a range of private and public sectors. She was also an active contributor to GHN's professional development, designing new coaching products and tools, a coaching competency framework and a coach induction programme and performance management system.

Lucy holds a BAC recognised diploma in person-centred counselling, as well as a diploma in communications, advertising and marketing.

Lucy can be reached at lucy.west@the coachingpartnership.co.uk.

Mike Milan's first career was in the public service. After university, he joined the Prison Service as Assistant Borstal Governor, was promoted to Deputy Governor, and subsequently to Staff College Tutor. Following this, he became headmaster of North Downs Approved School, before being appointed a social work inspector (policy advisor) in the Department of Health.

Mike's second career was in the private sector. In 1980, he became managing director of a Midlands optical chain, and seven years later its chairman. In 1982, he founded, with others, Social Information Systems, which went on to become the leading consultancy on the monitoring and evaluating of client delivery services within local authority social service departments and health authorities.

In the early 1990s, Mike sold his interest in both companies and sailed a small yacht to Greece and back. On his return, he joined GHN (now Penna Executive Coaching) as an executive coach. After two years, he became Director of Professional Development, responsible for managing and delivering the professional supervision of ten coaches and for the training of new coaches. While at GHN, Mike gained a BAC recognised diploma in person-centred counselling.

As a development coach, Mike has worked with senior executives, board members and chief executives in the private, public, voluntary and arts sectors.

Mike can be reached at mike.milan@thecoachingpartnership.co.uk.

Graham Alexander worked with IBM in line management and management development positions from 1967. He was then seconded to Operation Trident, a programme to give pupils the skills and experience to manage life after school. Graham then spent much of the 1970s researching and practising a variety of approaches to human performance and learning.

In 1979, he brought the coaching technology of the 'Inner Game' to Europe. He developed this methodology throughout the 1980s, playing a large part in bringing executive coaching on to corporate agendas. In 1986, Graham formed the Alexander Corporation Ltd, a market-leading consultancy which enabled some of the world's premier organisations to release and focus the human potential of their people. In 1999, Alexander merged with Sibson & Company (now Nextera).

Graham Alexander works with chief executives and executive teams to lead change and to enhance individual and collective effectiveness. He has worked extensively around the world in all market sectors, serving many of the FTSE 100 and Fortune 500 companies. Graham can be reached at galexander4@hotmail.com.

Beverly Brooks has been with Penna Executive Coaching (formerly GHN) since 1994 and specialises in intensive personalised change programmes. She has coached chief executives, main board directors and middle managers across a range of sectors and functions.

The main focus of her coaching activity is in preparing clients for higher leadership roles by exploring how they can be more effective in the way they operate. This entails a detailed look at the way individuals function and their assumptions about themselves, their business and their colleagues. Once patterns in behaviour are identified, these are then targeted for change in an intensive, focused programme which involves encouraging accurate self-observation and feedback. She is particularly interested in dealing with issues around control, authority and power in the leadership context, working to give clients greater self-awareness and thereby authentic leadership skills. Bev is a qualified Cognitive Analytic psychotherapist, a member of UKCP (United Kingdom Council for Psychotherapy) and ACAT (Association of Cognitive Analytic Therapy) and supervises the other coaches in her company. She can be reached at bev.brooks@virgin.net.

Myles Downey is a coach, consultant, author and speaker whose aim is to help others create work so that it is productive, fulfilling and a joy. He is Director of Studies at The School of Coaching in the UK, which he established in association with The Industrial Society, with the aim of developing the coaching capability of senior managers and executives.

Myles has worked with some of the most successful organisations in the Western hemisphere, across Europe, North and South America, Asia and in the CIS (Commonwealth of Independent States – former Soviet Union). He has significant experience in a variety of businesses, from professional service firms, banking, manufacturing, oil and gas, brewing and distilling, retailing and information technology. The predominant part of his work is in coaching senior executives and leadership teams. He is the author of *Effective Coaching* (Orion, 1999). Myles can be reached at myles@blueprint.co.uk.

Peter Fahrenkamp holds an MA in Organisational Development, and is the founder and principal of Pax Consulting, a US-based consultancy offering coaching, coach training, organisational development and facilitation services. Peter has incorporated Internet-based communication and collaboration tools into his work with clients in the US and Europe since 1993. Until 1997, he worked primarily as an executive coach with an international clientele of executives, business owners, managers and department heads in the public, educational and corporate sectors. Through contracts with one of the large international consultancies and other progressive US-based companies, Peter has focused on collaborative facilitated engagements and events since 1997. In this context, he has worked internationally with the leadership of many Fortune 500 companies. Peter was born in Germany and now lives in the USA. He works in both English and German and can be reached at Facilitation@Fahrenkamp.com.

Tony Ryan is Head of Executive Development at the BBC. This position was created at the beginning of 1998 to focus on the development and career planning of senior managers in the BBC. He has held a wide variety of HR roles in British Airways, IBM and BAA. Over the past ten years he has specialised in management development and succession planning, as Director of Executive Resources for IBM Europe and Director of Training and Management Development in BAA. He believes strongly in the principles of the 'Learning Organisation', and that this is highly relevant to the potential effectiveness of individual leaders. Tony can be reached at tonyryan@altavista.co.uk.

Glenn Whitney is the managing partner of ECD Insight, a management and communications development consultancy based in London. Glenn focuses on improving interpersonal communication through executive coaching, as well as leading dynamic and innovative programmes that develop emotional intelligence in teams and across organisations. He has been working for over ten years with senior executives from some of the world's most successful companies.

Trained in the US and the UK, Glenn has an MSc in Social Psychology (with distinction) from the London School of Economics and an MA in Counselling Psychology from City University and a BA in Psychology from Gettysburg College (Pennsylvania). He started his career as a business journalist, including seven years as a correspondent for the *Wall Street Journal*, where he jointly won the Overseas Press Club award for coverage of the Barings Bank collapse. He has lived and worked in several European cities as well as the US and speaks German, Spanish and French. Glenn can be reached at gwhitney@ecdinsight.com.

ACKNOWLEDGEMENTS

As well as our own views, this book contains the perspectives of many other people. We regret that lack of space prevents us from naming all those with whom we have spoken, but we would like to express our gratitude to everyone for their willingness to contribute. Our thanks, in particular, go to: David Peterson at PDI; Ben Cannon at Goldman Sachs; Jill Ader at Egon Zehnder; Mary Galbraith at PricewaterhouseCoopers; Anthony Saxton at Saxton Bamphylde; Chris Cooper, Robin Linnecar, Donald McLeod and Elizabeth Coffey at The Change Partnership and members of The Global Change Partnership, including Andy Johnson, Denise Fleming, Patricia Moroney, Julietta Lee, Kathy Strickland, Jesper Berggreen, John Harvey, Thierry Chavel, Iain Martin and Trevor Childs; our former colleagues at GHN (now Penna Executive Coaching), especially Terry Bates, Peter Gardiner-Hill and Peter Needham; and the following professional coaches: Karen McPherson, Patrick Allan, Gil Christie, Laura Whitworth and Judy Rosemarin.

We would also like to thank our six contributors and three clients (who formed the basis for the case studies) for their open and collaborative participation in the book. We are grateful to Stephen Rutt, at our publishers, for his support. Finally, we would like to thank our respective partners, Adrian West and Diane Milan, for their patience with us while we 'disappeared' into the book!

The authors and publisher are grateful for permission to use the following copyright material: Figure 1.2 from D. Kolb *Experiential Learning: Experience as the Source of Learning and Development.* Reprinted by permission of Pearson Education, Inc., Upper Saddle River, NJ.

Every effort has been made to trace all the copyright holders but if any have been inadvertently overlooked the publishers will be pleased to make the necessary arrangements at the first opportunity.

INTRODUCTION

Potential ... is not the demonstration of acquired assets but rather is the demonstration of the ability to acquire the assets needed for future situations ... In a world of rapid change, the real measure of leadership is the ability to acquire needed new skills as the situation changes.[1]

The Personal Challenge of Leadership

Over the past 20 years, the role of leadership has come to be seen as increasingly significant, and the requirement for the development of learning within organisations and the individuals heading them, more pressing. The leader occupies the position of most influence over the current effectiveness of the organisation and its future positioning. As rates of change accelerate, so the position of the business leader becomes more critical.

It is not surprising, therefore, that a substantial literature has grown up over this 20-year period on leadership. On the whole, this literature has focused on exhaustively describing the attributes and behaviour of effective leaders. In effect, much of the literature has been creating a gallery of role models from whom those in leadership positions may learn. This addresses the 'what' of leadership, but it does not address the 'how' of its acquisition. There is, in fact, very little written on the support and development of leadership for those already occupying senior positions; this book seeks to address that gap.

We believe that business leaders today have as their key role the knitting together of the rational and emotional, the content and process elements of their organisations. They need to do this to tackle head-on what has been so far an intractable issue in business: how to fully capitalise on the human assets – to consistently release, motivate and direct the potential of those who make up the organisation.

This is a matter of *personal* leadership. It implies an individual journey of development for the person occupying a leading role in a small or large organisation (although this becomes progressively more challenging as the scale of the organisation grows). It involves for that person integrating thinking and strategy with intuition and feeling in a process of occupying his or her role creatively, intelligently and authentically. We hope to demonstrate that what we shall be defining as 'professional coaching for leadership development' provides a unique vehicle for developing this leadership competency.

The Growth of Executive Coaching

In parallel with this growing focus on leadership has emerged the activity of executive coaching, first appearing in the early 1980s with one or two companies experimenting with this activity as part of their service portfolio. By the early 1990s, a nascent market had really started to gain momentum. Around 1995, a multitude of books by practitioner authors began to appear, mainly aimed at managers and leaders as coaches. Professional bodies like the International Coach Federation (ICF) took shape. The ICF held its first annual conference in 1995. The Consulting Psychology Division of the American Psychological Association devoted an entire issue of its journal to the subject of executive coaching in 1996. By 1998, there were at least four annual conferences devoted to coaching, and, at the time of writing (April 2001), we know of at least 30 books that have been published within the past 15 months.

The particular form of coaching that is the subject of this book, 'development coaching', has become more plainly visible over the past five years. By development coaching, we mean one-to-one consultancy with senior executives, which has as its objective the development of optimal effectiveness in a leadership and managerial role. It is an activity characterised by the creation of a structure in which the individual can stand back from his or her context, learn through a process of reviewing that context and his or her performance within it, and then act on that learning. This process becomes successful as a result of certain conditions offered and maintained by the coach. Perhaps the most important condition offered by the coach is that of providing accurate and authentic reflection of thinking and feeling. It is for that reason that we have called the book *The Reflecting Glass*.

The Aims of the Book

This book has the following aims:

- to provide a critical appreciation of the activity of development coaching

- to describe, demystify and benchmark this activity

- to make a case for its application to leadership learning

- to anticipate its future development

Our audience is, therefore, primarily those in leadership positions who are curious as to how this activity might help them (that is, chief executives and senior directors/executives), as well as those who seek to source external suppliers of this activity (for example chief executives and HR directors) and those already coaching or considering becoming development coaches themselves.

The Structure of the Book

We start by defining development coaching. We consider its genesis and the factors driving its demand, in particular, the need for a new form of leadership in the face of the current social and business climate. We then take the activity of development coaching and analyse its components so as to produce a practice model. We consider briefly theories of leadership in order to make our case for the unique relevance of this method of development to enhancing leadership of those at the top of organisations. In order to illustrate what we are saying, we describe our work with three particular leaders.

Next, we benchmark professional development coaching. We look at the process involved in contracting, managing the relationship with the employing organisation and managing the process of the work itself. Then we consider the skills involved in development coaching, where these may be drawn from and how they may be applied to leadership development. We end this review by looking at how these competencies might best be developed by those considering taking up this work.

We then stand back to review some of the key issues within professional coaching for leadership development. Three outside contributors look at the fundamental issues of evaluation, ethics and training. Glenn Whitney, a communications and management development coach, explores the issues of evaluating a 'soft' process in 'hard' terms. Beverly Brooks examines the ethical questions that development coaching needs to address, from her perspective as both a development coach and therapist in private practice. Myles Downey, a coach and coaching trainer who directs The School of Coaching at the Industrial Society describes the routes to training as a coach and models of coaching training.

This moves us forward to a future perspective. We look at the evolving market for development coaching and its increasing internationalisation, to set the scene for some futurology. Graham Alexander, one of the main architects of executive coaching in the UK, addresses the question of whether coaching is a fad, and considers the likely forms of its further development. Tony Ryan, the executive responsible for senior management development at the BBC, which has used coaching extensively, analyses the impact and the future likely take-up of coaching in this large organisation. Finally, Peter Fahrenkamp, a coach, management consultant and organisation development professional, considers the increasing influence that coaching is likely to have on the delivery of consulting and facilitation services more widely in the future.

Lastly, we return to the application of our assessment to practice. We look at the situation of the chief executives of large organisations and the dilemmas they face. We suggest how they may best explore the usefulness of coaching for themselves and take them through the criteria they should apply in selecting excellence in this service to them.

Appraising Coaching

As professional business coaches working with senior people, usually for a year or more, we have been curious and excited by the rapid development of the market for what we do. We are keen to attempt a critical appreciation of senior executive coaching and its place in the development of businesses and business leaders. This is a discipline that we believe can add substantial value to such development, but one that is very much at an emergent stage. The ability to establish an ethical base, quality standards and clear accountability will be key to its future credibility and take-up.

Our hope is that this book will contribute to the emerging debate, which accompanies the birth of any new profession. More particularly, we hope that it will help educate the market and increase the trend towards greater rigour.

We invite you, the reader, to be critical and enquiring as you read this book. We hope that, by the end of it, you will be able to answer for yourself these questions about professional coaching for leadership development:

- How does it work?

- Do I believe it does, or could, add value?

- Does it represent value for money for the substantial investment it comprises, and how do I assess this?

- How do I select for myself, or for my organisation, suppliers of excellence?

It is our hope that as a result of this enquiry process, you will gain greater clarity as to what this activity is, what its contribution to the development of your leadership might be and what rigour might look like, now and in the future.

Note

1. M.W. McCall Jr, *High Flyers: Developing the Next Generation of Leaders* (Boston: Harvard Business School Press, 1998) p. 5.

PART I

The Emerging Discipline of Professional Development Coaching

This book is about what we will be defining as 'professional development coaching', offered as a consultancy service to senior executives. Part I aims to put this form of coaching into its historical context. First, however, we distinguish broadly between the three main forms which executive coaching takes.

PART II

The Emerging Discipline
of Professional
Development Coaching

CHAPTER 1

Development Coaching Defined

Types of Coaching

We observe three types of coaching, as defined by:

- the client's development requirements
- the coaching objectives implied by those requirements
- the coaching response(s) appropriate to meet the objectives

These three types seem to fall along a continuum from 'training' to 'development', as illustrated in Figure 1.1.

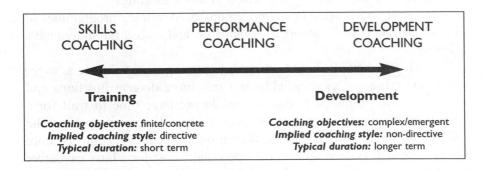

SKILLS COACHING	PERFORMANCE COACHING	DEVELOPMENT COACHING
Training		Development
Coaching objectives: finite/concrete *Implied coaching style:* directive *Typical duration:* short term		*Coaching objectives:* complex/emergent *Implied coaching style:* non-directive *Typical duration:* longer term

Figure 1.1 A training to development continuum of coaching

Skills Coaching

OBJECTIVES: 'Skills coaching' refers to where the client's development needs relate to developing specific skills and abilities, which define the coaching objectives clearly from the outset. This kind of coaching is sometimes also referred to as 'content coaching' or 'targeted coaching', involving best practice advice and training for specific skills, such as presenting, selling or dealing with the media.

THE COACH'S RESPONSE: Because the required skills are so specifically defined, it is possible, and efficient, for the coach to impart his or her expertise on the subject quite directively. In this mode, the coach is effectively training the client. What distinguishes skills coaching from traditional training is the fact that it is delivered one to one and can therefore be highly individualised. In this sense, it is similar to 'tutoring'.

In most traditional training programmes delivered in a group setting, *what* is being taught, as well as *how* it is being taught, are prescribed by the trainer. While there are varying degrees of participation and interaction during training programmes, there is not time for each individual to participate as fully as if he or she were the only trainee. The one-to-one setting of skills coaching allows for a two-way dialogue between coach and client in which the client can manage his or her own learning (for example expressing a preference for role playing or listening to the coach describe best practice).

While the timeframe for this individualised approach will depend upon the client's existing skills and the level he or she needs to attain, this type of focused coaching typically requires only a few meetings.

Skills coaching is often built into group-based training programmes to provide individualised support to personalise and embed the individual's learning.

This kind of individualised training is becoming more valuable as executives are promoted more quickly and into more diverse functions and situations than in the past. Executives do not have time to wait for a scheduled training programme or even to spend days away from the office. Although more expensive than training, skills coaching is more convenient and thus entails a lower opportunity cost for a busy executive since most skills coaches will be flexible enough to meet where and when the client wishes.

Performance Coaching

OBJECTIVES: As we move right on our continuum in Figure 1.1, the purpose of 'performance coaching' becomes wider in scope: to enhance a client's performance more generally in his or her current role, usually by enabling him or her to develop particular behaviours, or to remove blockages to his or her performance. It is sometimes also referred to as 'feedback coaching' since the required performance improvement is often identified in the context of a development planning process, or, more commonly, as the result of a '360-degree' feedback process.

The term '360-degree' refers to the process of surveying relevant people whose roles surround that of the particular coaching client in the organisational hierarchy. These would typically include the executive's subordinates, possibly a selection of *their* subordinates, a selection of the executive's peers, the executive's boss(es) and possibly his or her boss's boss.

People at work are generally capable of a great deal more than their current performance. Performance coaching provides an opportunity to unlock personal potential and/or address underperformance. If an individual is not giving 100% of him or herself at work, it is often because the 'psychological contract' between the individual and boss or other colleagues is out of alignment. One of the most common agenda items we encounter is lack of clarity of expectations between individuals and their stakeholders (especially their boss). Performance coaching can provide the space for an individual to unravel his or her own set of assumptions and then plan to compare and negotiate expectations with his or her stakeholders more transparently.

THE COACH'S RESPONSE: Since the client's development requirements and the implied coaching objectives are less precisely defined than in the case of skills coaching, the performance coach's response needs to be more flexible than with skills coaching.

Typically, the performance coach will engage the organisational sponsor (usually the individual's line manager and/or an HR professional) more actively in the early stages of the referral. The performance coach will request a briefing, either with or without the client present. Sometimes the reason for the referral is largely contextual (most commonly, the individual is moving into a new role). When the reason for the referral is more specific to the individual's current performance or behaviour, the organisation is usually fairly clear about how it wishes the client to develop. However, where there is considered to be underperformance, the degree to which this has been communicated to the client varies greatly. It often transpires that the individual's boss is uncomfortable giving direct feedback to the individual, and that there is a tacit hope that coaching will deliver the bad news instead. In these cases, the coach's first role is to facilitate transparent communication between the boss and client so that expectations are clear.

It is worth noting that even with direct feedback, prospective clients have varying degrees of motivation to participate in coaching, and to be open to the change involved. They may feel pressured to accept the offer of coaching lest they do not appear open to such change, but privately they may feel wary or suspicious of the prospect. The first performance coaching sessions therefore focus upon enlisting the client's active participation, without which his or her coaching will not succeed.

Performance coaching typically runs over a period of three to six months. During early scoping of the coaching work, the coach often has to manage the organisation's expectations about how much, and what type of, development or change is realistic within the available timeframe.

Since the agenda will have been focused around clearly defined performance objectives in the first few sessions, the coach plays a fairly directive role in 'keeping the client on track'. Sessions are likely to follow the agenda quite closely, without much deviation on to other topics (although there is more flexibility than with skills coaching). When it comes to the particular issues within the agenda, however, the coach will play a less directive role, facilitating the client's own exploration of each issue and conclusions regarding what action he or she believes should be taken.

A model that can be used to launch the performance coaching process is provided in Box 1.1.

While all corporately sponsored coaching needs to address both the individual and organisational agendas, performance coaching places a slightly greater priority upon the organisational agenda than we will see in 'development coaching'. The raison d'être for performance coaching is that an organisation wants an individual to extend his or her 'behavioural repertoire' in order to enhance his or her individual performance and thus the organisation's performance. This is reflected in the fact that most performance coaching referrals are initiated by the organisation. While the client will benefit personally from this process, this is not the primary purpose of the investment.

Performance coaching has experienced a shift over the last few years, away from an initially remedial connotation. Executives were initially referred clandestinely to coaches, implying that both the organisation and the individual regarded the process as a sign of underperformance or weakness. More recently, there are an increasing number of executives who are proud to declare they are seeing a coach because it signifies that their organisation is prepared to make a substantial investment in them.

Box 1.1

1. Define current role
   - Objectives/responsibilities
   - Assessment of value (and non value) added activities
   - Opportunities for greater delegation of non value added activities, to free up time for ...

2. Define 'excellence in role'

   In individual role:
   - Task related (for example scope for more added value 'task' contributions)
   - Relationship related (for example developing people, succession planning)

   In team membership role, for example:
   - Vision/innovation/ideas generation
   - Structure/process improvement
   - Communication/facilitation (within and between meetings)

   In any other role/capacity (for example project manager of new initiative)

3. Feedback/relationship-building process
   - Define 5–10 stakeholders (from whom to seek 360-degree feedback)
   - Solicit feedback from stakeholders (for example a simple 'three strengths and three weaknesses' format to limit time required of respondent and to provide focus for the individual)
   - Coach collates responses (thus ensuring anonymity)
   - Address feedback themes and identify approach for addressing development needs
   - Return to stakeholders to explore themes and build relationships around sharing of development

Because of its focus on results in a shorter timeframe, organisations are especially attracted to performance coaching. It can also be easier to gain acceptance from busy executives themselves, who feel more comfortable devoting time to their own development when they feel confident of quick results.

Development Coaching

OBJECTIVES: On the right of the continuum in Figure 1.1 is 'development coaching', which is the focus of this book. The development coaching task is to create the conditions for reflective learning. A coach does this by first creating a psychological space, which allows the executive to stand back from the workplace, and then providing a supportive, yet challenging, relationship and dialogue in which the executive can gain perspective on his or her experiences and self, and on his or her leadership task within the organisation.

The nature of this dialogue has its roots in David A. Kolb's learning theory, illustrated in Figure 1.2.

Kolb identified that individuals maximise their learning by working through a cycle of:

- experiencing

- reflecting on the experience

- drawing conclusions or theories about what that experience means

- planning to test out that learning the next time they encounter the same experience

Research by learning experts, Mumford and Honey, has demonstrated that individuals tend to have preferences for one of these four elements of

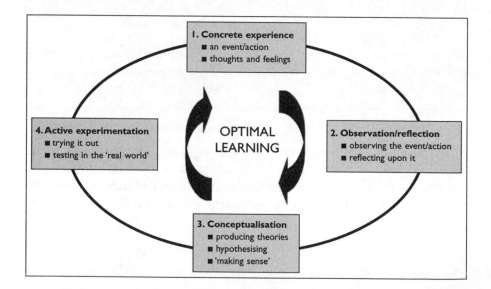

Figure 1.2 Kolb's learning cycle

(adapted from D. Kolb, by permission of Pearson Education, Inc.)

learning, but that everyone learns the most from working through the full cycle.[1] Development coaching provides the structure and setting for the individual to learn in this reflective way.

While development coaching is appropriate for anyone, it adds the most value to the organisation when it is offered to senior executives as their roles involve managing considerable complexity and a wide span of discretion. Further, they exercise a substantial influence on the rest of the organisation.

To address this complexity and its concomitant challenges, development coaching requires a longer term investment on the parts of both the organisation and the individual. While skills and performance coaching are essentially focused on the short term (that is, usually looking at a one-year horizon), development coaching tends to look at a one- to five-year horizon. The process helps the client to develop a detailed understanding of his or her situation and role, to articulate a personal and business strategy and to apply the action arising from this over the next two or three years in the context of his or her longer term career.

The objectives of development coaching are more client defined than with skills and performance coaching. Since development coaching clients are typically more senior, there is a greater coincidence between their interests and those of their organisations than with more junior clients. Indeed, many development coaching clients pay for the coaching out of their own budgets. Even where there is a separate organisational sponsor, the sponsor has to respect and trust the client to use the experience in a way that balances the organisational and individual interests. If feedback to such a sponsor is required, it is likely to cover progress towards agreed objectives, rather than the processes and detail of the coaching programme (that is, the 'what' rather than the 'how').

Development coaching is highly individualised. Skills and performance coaching tend to operate with either explicit or implicit reference to a common set of competencies or preferred behaviour, while a development coach meets an individual with little preconceived notions of what his or her response to the environment should be. Because development coaching is helping senior executives to develop the capacity to define their *own* view of successful personal and corporate performance, and strategy flowing from this, it is clearly inappropriate for the coach to interject a preconceived notion of what optimal behaviour or strategy should be.

THE COACH'S RESPONSE: Development coaching takes an holistic approach to the individual, recognising that reflective learning crosses over professional and personal boundaries. It embraces wider influences on individual behaviour, from all elements of a client's current and past, personal and professional lives.

Development coaching is a more emergent process than skills or performance coaching. The process begins by identifying the agenda and development goals, but, more often than not, the agenda alters depending on changing circumstances in the client's world.

However, while development coaching may emerge in a way that maximises its flexibility and helpfulness to the client, it should also be a managed process. Regular review sessions are built in for the coach and the client to reflect on the work they have done and its relationship to their agreed agenda.

The type of relationship implied by development coaching is of an equal partnership. The client is recognised to be expert in his or her field, while the coach is expert in providing the necessary conditions for the client's learning.

Development coaching typically lasts for 12 to 18 months, although coaching relationships can last for years. Clear contracting and re-contracting should be undertaken at regular intervals to ensure that the focus of the coaching is still appropriate, and the investment of time and money remains justified.

Three Dimensions of Development Coaching

We consider now three dimensions of development coaching: professionalism, purpose, and the central place of the relationship between coach and client. In our view, a proper understanding of the nature of these is essential to the successful delivery of development coaching.

Professionalism

Professionalism in development coaching will include at least the following elements:

Being objective/disinterested
The coach should be able to maintain neutrality and transparency, offering clear and focused reflection of his or her client's thinking and feeling. It is important, therefore, that he or she keeps in place the boundaries and personal support to maintain this neutrality and objectivity. It also means that the coach needs to be explicit about times when he or she may wish to 'stretch the boundaries' of the coaching role (for example when offering advice, which is actually operating in a more traditional consulting role).

Clear contracting
In development coaching the relationship is often triangular, with the company sponsoring the client, being, as it were, an equal or secondary client. Since the sponsoring organisations fund coaching, they can reasonably expect that their objectives and views of the client's working situation influence the coaching work. As we described earlier, in performance coaching that influence may largely define the agenda; in development coaching a more even balance is held. This represents a challenge to the coach in maintaining his or her professional integrity towards an individual client while remaining accountable to both the client and sponsoring organisation. This implies open negotiation and the boundaries agreed being maintained rigorously (we describe this in detail in Chapters 5 and 6).

Supported by explicit standards of conduct
These may include:

- demonstrating professional rigour underpinned by full session notes and a focus on results

- holding a proper balance between corporate and individual interests

- maintaining transparent processes and open communication with all parties

- maintaining a researched referral network for related services (for example psychometric assessment, team facilitation, media/presentation training, outplacement, counselling)

- demonstrating a formal and reliable means of monitoring and reporting on progress of the contract

Founded on an ethical base
This means guaranteeing confidentiality with regard to personal information from coaching sessions (within the agreed limits of the contract) and with regard to information about the company gleaned as a result of coaching. In our own practice, we are specifically debarred from acting upon information so gained and regard ourselves as 'insiders'.

Committed to ongoing personal and professional development
This means that the coach should have a structure in place to extend his or her own ability to empathise with the client and the client's situation and to extend his or her knowledge and understanding of the context of organisational and business life. We will elaborate upon this in Chapter 6.

Purpose

Coaching is an activity with a 'hard' purpose. It seeks to enable the individual leader to increase his or her impact and contribution and should subject itself to scrutiny of its outputs.

The purpose of coaching varies in terms of the context within which the coaching takes place (for example level of management of the individual, nature of role or job, nature of transition being faced or of the organisational change). But, in any context, the task of coaching is to help the individual to adapt congruently and therefore creatively and innovatively to the challenges involved. If that adaptation is inhibited so that the individual is unable to function optimally, then coaching may address the 'blockage' in order to clear the way towards greater performance. (If that blockage is deep seated, then it may be appropriate to refer the client to therapy, after which he or she may return to coaching to complete the developmental task as originally agreed upon.)

The main outputs of development coaching are:

- the development of perspective (making sense of, or patterning, reality as a result of forming a clear point of view) and taking action in the light of it

- increasing the capacity for dealing with complexity and ambiguity

- the development of a flexible 'repertoire' of behaviour, enabling adaptation and a versatility of responding to different circumstances

The Relationship

The relationship between the coach and client is central to the success of the coaching process. When a client selects a development coach, he or she is choosing a relationship with an individual, not a service from an organisation. The relationship is the vehicle for the work and any technology or tools offered as part of the coaching process are simply there to provide material for reflection, or support the focus and purpose of the contract.

The coaching relationship represents a collaboration between two people with the goal of a growth in self-awareness and functioning of the client as the common objective of both. In this collaboration, the development coach provides the learning context, while the client, usually a highly able and well-functioning leader, brings his or her understanding and knowledge of context to the enquiry. The relationship is essentially one in which power is equal. Indeed, we believe that a view of coaching based on the idea of a coach as guru or expert is unhelpful.

Summary

Table 1.1 summarises the key characteristics of each type of coaching.

In reality, there is, of course, overlap between the three types of coaching. Our categorisation is intended to indicate the *primary* focus of the coaching in question rather than to imply that the categories are sharply boundaried. Even with a development coaching client, a coach may at times find him or herself in performance or skills coaching mode.

However, despite these likely overlaps, it is advisable that the coach clarify with the sponsor the primary type of coaching being sought and how he or she would propose meeting that need. In addition, coaches who are offering all three types should be transparent with the client about which mode(s) they are operating in at any one time.

In Chapter 2, we move on to consider the factors that have influenced the emergence of development coaching as a professional discipline.

Note

1. P. Honey and A. Mumford, *Using Your Learning Styles* (Maidenhead: Peter Honey Publications, 1983).

Table 1.1 Key characteristics of types of coaching

Type of Coaching	Typical Agenda Issues	Coach Role/Style	Contracting and Feedback	Typical Duration and Frequency of Meetings
Skills	Just-in-time skills, for example for presentations, dealing with the media, negotiating Individual support following a training programme to embed learning and apply it to the workplace	Skills expert Directive style	Clear goals and simple contracting Review and feed back to sponsor at the end (from client and coach)	2–3 two-hour meetings over 1–2 months
Performance	Clarifying expected performance in current role or project Maximising performance in a current role or project Changing behaviours based upon feedback Preparing for a new role (for example functional to general management promotion) Support during induction to new organisation Support during change initiative	Mixture of expert and facilitator Directive management of programme and non-directive style of coaching	Contracting required to agree goals and align expectations Review and feed back to sponsor at the end (from client and coach)	Weekly or fortnightly one-hour meetings over 3–6 months
Development	Rich analysis of current organisation and of managerial/leadership objectives Planning and implementing personal and business strategy in light of these Identifying strengths and weaknesses in personal performance (through self-reflection and/or feedback) and developing in response Planning for next role and identifying development needs Charting future career over 1–5 years	Non-directive, partnership approach Sounding board	Complex contracting to establish agenda Regular re-contracting to reflect changing circumstances/priorities Nature and frequency of reviews and feedback to sponsor agreed as part of contracting	One-and-a-half-hour meetings every 2–4 weeks over 6–18 months

CHAPTER 2

The Supply and Demand Factors

In order to understand what we are calling 'professional development coaching' today and its potential future, it is useful to review the context in which it has arisen. As with the emergence of any new market, there seem to be supply and demand factors, which have led to its genesis.

Appendix 1 maps the more general terrain of coaching from which professional development coaching has emerged.

The Supply Factors

Executive coaching has been practised for much longer than it has been named 'coaching'. Many consultants, trainers and other related professionals claim to have been coaching for years, although, in most cases, before they called their service 'coaching'. Three of the earliest examples of formal executive coaching programmes which we came across in our research date to around 1981. Personnel Decisions International (PDI), based in the US, began offering their 'Individual Coaching for Effectiveness' programme, and in the UK, Jinny Ditzler and Graham Alexander started a company called Results Unlimited, providing a structured coaching programme focused around increasing work–life results and enhancing well-being. In parallel with the latter, Graham Alexander co-led a UK business with Sir John Whitmore called The Inner Game, which, by the early 1980s, was also offering one-to-one coaching specifically for managers and training and management development personnel.

Despite these earlier origins, we mark the genesis of *professional development coaching* as around 1987, the time when a service of the kind we described in Chapter 1 and Appendix 1 (that is, a one-to-one, externally provided service paid for by an organisation for the purpose of developing its leaders) began to be *commonly*, and *formally*, described as executive coaching by both professionals offering, and clients seeking, such a service.

It is a common perception that executive coaching more generally originated in the US. However, from our research, we have concluded that there was a parallel development in both the US and the UK. While there appears to have been little cross-fertilisation between the two countries during the first half of the 1990s, there was a very similar convergence of various streams of influence in each country leading up to and during that time. These 'streams' fall into three categories, which influenced the supply of executive coaching, and more specifically, what we have defined as development coaching:

- The role of psychology
- Social trends
- Business trends

The Role of Psychology

The application of the study of human behaviour and psychology to the workplace has a long history, of which executive coaching is one of the more recent chapters. Some understanding of this history is important to an appreciation of coaching.

For most of the 20th century, psychologists were consulted by companies to provide insight into employee motivations and abilities. The two main applications of psychology have been:

- *recruitment and selection* (that is, testing, often with psychometric instruments, to make sure an employer hires the right employees)
- *assessment* (that is, evaluating, often at off-site assessment centres, existing employees, either to select them for future roles or inclusion in a 'top management cadre' and/or to identify their development needs)

As psychologists were already being used to assess managers' skills and behaviours in these ways, they began to be asked by line managers and HR professionals to follow through with *developing* managers in the areas in which they had been assessed as weaker.

Some pioneering executive search companies experimented with combining psychological assessment and coaching in the late 1980s. Typically, the psychologist would assess the client (usually using a combination of psychometric testing and interview-based assessment) and then debrief the client with the coach present as a 'handover' (sometimes with the client's boss present, as well). The coach and client would then continue their work together, addressing the areas identified in the assessment process.

A second, more recent wave of psychologists entering the coaching market came as a result of the changes in the healthcare systems in the US and Australia during the 1990s. As national healthcare budgets came under increasing scrutiny and suffered reductions, psychologists practising within the public sector found themselves out of jobs. Books such as *From Couch to Corporation*, by psychotherapist and business consultant, Iris Martin, encouraged and guided therapists and psychologists to transfer their skills to executive coaching.[1]

Social Trends

The growth of executive coaching, seen in a wider cultural context, has also been influenced by various social trends over the past few decades.

The Personal Development Movement

The American-originated 'human potential movement' started in the 1960s and has grown rapidly. Personal development organisations such as EST (now Landmark Forum) and The Esalen Institute, talk shows such as *Oprah* and self-help gurus such as Anthony Robbins and Stephen Covey, have further heightened an appetite for self-exploration and personal development in the US and, increasingly, elsewhere in the world. Most of these phenomena have their roots in the 'American dream' and 'can-do' philosophy, values that the Baby Boomer generation, in particular, adopted with enthusiasm.

Thomas Leonard is widely credited as one of the early pioneers of personal, or life coaching, in the US. He began his own life coaching practice (initially based on personal financial planning) in 1982. More significantly, he stimulated a huge increase in the volume of coaches by starting the first 'coach-the-coach' training programme with Coach University in 1989. This, in turn, led to the founding of the International Coach Federation (ICF) in 1992, which has become the leading professional association for personal and executive coaches. The ICF provides credentialling and referral programmes for its members. At the time of writing, the ICF has 4,000 members in 26 countries. In the last 18 months, the ICF has noticed a substantial increase in interest, including a doubling of membership enquiries each month. Its annual conferences have been selling out and the ICF had to double the capacity of the 2001 conference (to 2,500).

In the last couple of years, life coaching (see Appendix 1 for further information) has spread to the UK and Australia, and this area looks likely to grow substantially. Frederic Hudson, in his *Handbook of Coaching*, attributes this growth to more recent social issues:

> I see the new profession of adult coaching as a partial remedy for the cultural crisis we are undergoing today – a crisis due, in part, to our bewilderment over changes in the rules that govern our lives. Many rules we had counted on to keep us on a steady course in life no longer apply ... those rules could only work in a culture high in continuity, control and agreed-upon authority.[2]

The Sports Analogy

Another wider social influence upon the rise of coaching has come from the sporting world. The active use of the sports analogy seems to have arisen first in the UK, where, in the late 1980s, the concept of coaching in sport was transferred to business. The American tennis coach, Tim Gallwey, had written a book called *The Inner Game of Tennis* in 1974. His use of the word 'inner' espoused a more holistic and implicitly psychological approach to sporting performance. He referred to concepts such as achieving a 'peak performance' or experience of 'flow'.

Later encapsulated as the equation of 'Performance = Potential – Interference',[3] Gallwey expressed his belief that the opponent within one's own head is more formidable than the one the other side of the net. He argued that sports professionals could benefit from increased self-awareness which would, in turn, lead to less interference with, and anxiety about, their own performance. Gallwey's approach was radical at the time for the traditional sports coaching field based on instruction. By the early 1980s, a small circle of sports coaches in the UK using Gallwey's principles found their clients, who happened also to be business executives, asking the coaches to apply their approach to both the clients' personal and professional lives.

Gallwey has recently published *The Inner Game of Work* (2000), which widens his original theories developed in sports coaching to the world of work for non-athletes. He states that 'one of the biggest problems in the modern corporate environment is the breakdown of trust in the individual'[4] and advocates that 'perhaps the greatest benefit the Inner Game coach brings to the conversation is to trust clients more than the clients trust themselves'.[5] And, he adds, 'having that trust in the client can be achieved only by [the coach] having learned an increasingly profound trust in oneself'.[6]

His description of 'Inner Game coaching' offers a good definition of development coaching:

> Effective coaching in the workplace holds a mirror up for clients, so they can see their own thinking process. As a coach, I am not listening for the content of what is being said as much as I am listening to the way they are thinking, including how their attention is focused and how they define the key elements of the situation.[7]

Gallwey's thesis is founded upon the concept that people most critically need help getting out of their own way and minimising their own 'interference'. He states that 'coaching can be viewed not so much as a process of *adding* as it is a process of *subtracting*, or *unlearning* whatever is getting in the way of movement toward the client's desired goal'.[8]

In 1984, Graham Alexander, in working with one of The Inner Game's corporate clients (a world-leading professional service firm), developed the 'GROW' (for 'goal, reality, options, wrap-up') model from Gallwey's original thinking. This model is widely used by many coaches today and may be the most prevalent coaching model.

In 1992, Sir John Whitmore, a car racing champion, published *Coaching for Performance*. Along with Alexander, Whitmore had been a key player in the sports circle described above. In his book, he re-presented the GROW (now standing for 'goal–reality–options–*will*') model. While an increasing number of books on coaching were starting to appear on the scene in the US and UK by this time, most of them were aimed at helping managers to adopt a 'coaching style of management'. Although Whitmore stated in his book that a wider audience of business managers and HR professionals could certainly benefit from the same principles, he was one of the first, if not *the* first, to mention the concept of an 'independent [business] coach' in print.[9]

The sporting analogy is still widely used among executive coaches to claim that business people can benefit from the same type of relationship which top athletes have long used to realise their potential. A particular lesson from this analogy is that sports coaches do not have to be as talented as the athletes they coach (just as a business coach does not have to know a client's business or role better than the client). Coaching in whatever context is about *facilitating* the client's enhanced performance.

Business Trends

Outplacement and Career Management

During the 1980s and early 1990s, large swathes of redundancies were created in the drive towards greater business efficiency. 'Outplacement' became a new industry in response to these mass redundancies. Outplacement consultants were most commonly occupational psychologists and career counsellors. As they worked with large numbers of employees who had been made redundant, some outplacement professionals began to identify the costs of 'throwing the baby out with the bathwater'. They advised their corporate clients that, while the company might be making short-term cost efficiencies by eliminating redundant positions or parting company with underperforming individuals, they were also losing valuable skills and intellectual capital in the form of individuals with long histories with the company in the process.

As the more entrepreneurial outplacement companies in both the US and UK saw the opportunity for a 'line extension' to their service, they started to advocate to their corporate clients the benefits of what some called 'insourcing'. These outplacement professionals worked with companies to identify talented executives who were struggling during the upheavals of downsizing, and to support them to remain, and, moreover, rejuvenate their careers, within their existing organisations.

A few companies even set up specifically to offer this service. In the UK for example, two experienced businessmen, Peter Gardiner-Hill and Peter Needham, teamed up to form a company called GHN in 1981. Although not sports coaches themselves, Gardiner-Hill and Needham drew upon the sports analogy to convince organisations that senior executives had more potential than they realised and would be cheaper to develop than to replace. In particular, they advocated proactive career management, promoting such concepts as 'Me plc', the notion that executives should manage their own careers like they manage their businesses.

But outplacement companies, and even those such as GHN who had never explicitly offered outplacement, faced a challenge in distinguishing themselves from pure outplacement. There was a conflict in connotations between perceived failure (for example victims of redundancies were sometimes brutally referred to as 'damaged goods') and success (that is, developing prized talent). Clients sent to career counsellors at outplacement firms for development purposes were anxious that there might be, or be perceived to be, a hidden agenda. And there often was, as companies started to use career counselling as a final opportunity to rectify problems (for which the prognosis was probably not good).

The outplacement companies who attempted to make the transition from outplacement to coaching providers during the mid-1990s generally did so in two ways:

1. By completely leaving behind their outplacement service in order to escape the remedial connotation of career counselling and outplacement. In many cases, former outplacement companies have quietly maintained a small proportion of outplacement work for commercial reasons (that is, they don't want to turn down business), but they play it down to avoid jeopardising their coaching image.

2. Fully diversifying into an HR consultancy, offering a range of services to cover all stages of the employment life cycle, from recruitment/ search to training and development and performance management to outplacement. Increasing numbers of HR consultancies now offer some form of executive coaching. We will be describing some of the operating challenges of offering coaching within a wider consultancy context in Chapter 10.

The Demand Factors

In many ways mirroring these supply factors, we believe that the past five years' explosion in coaching activity is also the result of more endemic demand factors within business, stemming back at least 20 years and including:

- The diminishing of corporate and individual security

- The growing imperative for continuous organisational and individual learning

- The need for new leadership

The Diminishing of Corporate and Individual Security

In the early 1980s, Western business became concerned about its increasing lack of competitiveness, especially compared to the growing Japanese economy. By the time the US slipped into recession in the early 1990s, the corporate appetite for a solution to the continuing competitive struggle was eager for a new approach; this came in the form of 'business process reengineering' (BPR). As described by Stuart Crainer in *The Management Century:*

The beauty of reengineering was that it embraced many of the fashionable business ideas of recent years and nudged them forward into a tidy philosophy. There were strains of total quality management, just-in-time manufacturing, customer service, time-based competition and lean manufacturing in the reengineering concept.[10]

BPR advocated cost reduction through efficiency gains and what came to be known as 'corporate downsizing'. Although this rational approach sounded attractive in theory, it overlooked the human dimension of such radical change. As mentioned earlier, efficiency savings translated into huge numbers of employees being made redundant and the birth of outplacement to help executives leave their companies and find a new job. While those made redundant suffered, even those who were not experienced a sense of insecurity in the face of the breakdown of the traditional psychological contract (that is, 'a job for life'). Executives woke up to the fact that they could no longer rely on job security and needed to manage their own careers.

There was an organisational cost, as well. Organisations were stripped down to the bare bones, and terms like 'corporate anorexia' warned of the dangers of crippling organisational capability. By stripping out not only the 'fat' of operational inefficiencies, but also the 'muscle' of essential resources and skills, organisations left surviving managers overloaded, distracted and distrustful. In a study of top-quintile firms in a report by Sibson & Co (now Nextera) and McKinsey in 1998, 75% described their companies as 'fast-paced and high-stress environments' (*Sibson & Co corporate magazine* **ix**(1)).

This additional stress in corporate life has become one of the drivers in the growth of executive coaching. As *Fortune* magazine described in February 2000:

> It's not that executive coaching is particularly new. But in the past five years, coaching has gone mass-market. In the age of Every Man for Himself, every man can have a coach – and, in an ever-more-commonly-held view, needs one.[11]

The Growing Imperative for Continuous Organisational and Individual Learning

As competition intensified throughout the 1990s, customers sensed their growing power and became more demanding. Companies sought to differentiate themselves in the eyes of their customers and began to focus on their 'core competencies'. Moreover, they began to realise that as soon as they came up with one competitive advantage, it would be copied by their competitors and their customers would just demand more.

Business commentators began to remark upon the phenomenon of constant and accelerating change and the need for organisations to develop the capacity for reinventing themselves by continually innovating. While reengineering had required sophisticated analytical and numerical skills, constant innovation required something more intangible: the ability for organisations to continually adapt and learn. This, in turn, created an increasing focus on the business or 'human assets' that are contained within individuals. Although there has historically been an aversion to tackling such ambiguous, complex and intangible issues, the business case for organisational and individual development is becoming strong.

Arie de Geus and Peter Senge state in *The Living Company*, their book about what characteristics companies who have endured the test of time share, that 'your ability to learn faster than your competition is your only sustainable competitive advantage'.[12] Indeed, there is a growing body of evidence to suggest that companies that manage their people assets better and invest in becoming 'learning organisations' are outstripping their competitors. The Sibson and McKinsey report mentioned earlier indicated that:

> firms with more capable people at the top have a 70% higher total return to shareholders. The study discovered that companies in the top-quintile of shareholder return reported having stronger talent and talent management practices than those in the mid-quintile. *Fortune* magazine's 1999 list of 100 Best Companies to Work For indicated that paying attention to the personal and professional needs of workers is good for business. Those companies thought best to work for and which have been publicly traded for a minimum of five years, experienced an average stock appreciation of 25% for that period compared with a 19% gain by the Russell 2000 index. (*Sibson & Co corporate magazine* **ix**(1): 6)

Daniel Goleman cites research in his book, *Working with Emotional Intelligence*, from a project sponsored by the Society for Human Resource Management at the Saratoga Institute:

> Since 1986, the institute has collected data from nearly six hundred companies in more than twenty industries, detailing policies and practices. They analysed top companies, selected for profitability, cycle times, volume, and other similar indices of performance. Searching for what these outstanding companies held in common, the institute identified the following basic practices in managing 'human assets' – their people:

- A balance between the human and financial sides of the company's agenda
- Organisational commitment to a basic strategy
- Initiatives to stimulate improvements in performance
- Open communication and trust-building with all stakeholders
- Building relationships inside and outside that offer competitive advantage
- Collaboration, support and sharing resources
- Innovation, risk taking, and learning together
- A passion for competition and continual improvement[13]

Thus, there is a growing appreciation that employees represent a financial investment to be optimised rather than a cost to be minimised. Although the intangible nature of these assets makes measurement more difficult, 'human capital' is rapidly becoming a relevant and important metric of company value. And the measures of human capital return are changing dramatically, from the single-efficiency metrics of the industrial era (for example manufacturing throughput times) to qualitative customer satisfaction measures (for example loyalty and intimacy).

The Need for New Leadership

This growing imperative for organisational and individual learning in turn implies the need for a new form of leadership. The notion of leadership that derives its authority from a 'command and control' model does not work in a world that has become substantively unpredictable. The uncertainty and insecurity described above encourages employees to look to leaders whose authority comes not from the position they hold in the hierarchy, but from their ability to articulate an idea of the organisation and gain buy-in for that idea through a process of open dialogue with members of the organisation. As Warren Bennis states in his book, *On Becoming a Leader*, 'the challenge of leadership is to create the social architecture where ideas, relationships and adventure can flourish'.[14] Bennis identified four common abilities from a study of 90 leaders as:

- management of attention
- management of meaning
- management of trust
- management of self[15]

Bennis defined leadership most of all by 'management of attention', which he described as 'the capacity to create a compelling vision and translate it into action and sustain it'.[16] 'Management of meaning' referred to the effective communication skills required to elicit that attention in others, including the use of visionary language expressed with inspirational emotion. Bennis described the 'management of trust' as 'the emotional glue that binds followers and leaders together'.[17] Finally, the 'management of self' requires the genuine self-confidence that comes from self-knowledge, and that enables the determination and courage to take risks.

This implies a very demanding role. If leaders are to perform it successfully, they will need development in the skills implied.

A very considerable literature has been produced on the subject of this leadership challenge over the past five to ten years. Yet, virtually all of it has been devoted to *defining* leadership – *what* and *who* leaders should become. Very little has been written about *how* leaders can develop the skills and attributes outlined. As McCall describes in *High Flyers*:

> There is apparently a widespread and fundamental need to believe that a single (and usually short) list of generic qualities can be used to describe all effective leaders and that these qualities are relatively stable over the course of a person's career. It is much more manageable, after all, to search for only one set of attributes than to contend with the possibility that people with quite different attributes might be equally effective or that people might change over time for the better or for the worse as a result of their experiences.[18]

Indeed, from all this discussion about what leaders should become, we believe that there is a growing appreciation on the part of people in senior positions that they may need support in identifying how to respond. According to a study by PricewaterhouseCoopers, chief executives of some of America's fastest-growing companies are increasingly holding up a mirror to themselves. The study involved interviews with chief executives of 441 product and service companies identified as the fastest growing US businesses. Of the chief executives surveyed, 32% said their own ability to manage or reorganise their business could be 'an impediment to growth' during the next 12 months, compared to seven years ago when only 10% of those surveyed said they felt this way.[19]

Summary

In this chapter, we have looked at the supply and demand factors behind the emergence of professional development coaching. We have drawn attention to the focus on leadership that has developed in parallel to the substantial changes in business life over the past 10 to 20 years, and the resultant and pressing need for creative leadership. We believe that a main factor in the future growth of coaching at the top of organisations will be that it can provide a possibly unique context for individuals in leadership positions to address their development. We explore this claim in the next chapter.

Notes

1. I. Martin, *From Couch to Corporation: Becoming a Successful Corporate Therapist* (New York: John Wiley & Sons, 1996).
2. F.M. Hudson, *The Handbook of Coaching* (San Francisco: Jossey-Bass, 1999) p. xvii.
3. W.T. Gallwey, *The Inner Game of Work*, 2nd edn (London: Orion Business Book, 2000) p. 17.
4. Ibid., p. 194.
5. Ibid., p. 193.
6. Ibid., p. 193.
7. Ibid., p. 182.
8. Ibid.,. p. 210.
9. J. Whitmore, *Coaching for Performance* (London: Nicholas Brealey, 1996) p. 3.
10. S. Crainer, *The Management Century: A Critical Review of 20th Century Thought and Practice* (San Francisco: Jossey-Bass, 2000) p. 186.
11. B. Morris, 'So You're a Player, Do You Need a Coach?', *Fortune*, **141** (21 February, 2000) p. 144.
12. A. de Geus and P.M. Senge, *The Living Company* (Boston: Harvard Business School Press, 1997).
13. Quoted in D. Goleman, *Working with Emotional Intelligence* (London: Bloomsbury, 1998) p. 301.
14. W. Bennis, *On Becoming a Leader* (Reading, MA: Perseus Books, 1994) p. xiv.
15. Quoted in S. Crainer, *The Management Century: A Critical Review of 20th Century Thought and Practice* (San Francisco: Jossey-Bass, 2000) p. 180.
16. Ibid., p. 180.
17. Ibid., p. 180.
18. M.W. McCall Jr., *High Flyers: Developing the Next Generation of Leaders* (Boston: Harvard Business School Press, 1998) p. xi.
19. 'More Entrepreneurs Take Help of Executive Coaches: CEOs Hope to Gain', *Wall Street Journal*, 9 May 2000.

PART II

A Framework for Professional Coaching for Leadership Development

The focus of Part II is on the practice of development coaching. In Chapter 3, we present a model for this form of coaching and consider its application to developing leadership. In Chapter 4, we illustrate coaching with leaders facing three different challenges. In Chapter 5, we outline the processes involved in the delivery of professional development coaching and, in Chapter 6, we review the competencies required of the coach undertaking this work.

Development Coaching: A Model

A Marriage of Two Disciplines

We believe that the development coach draws on two related disciplines (as illustrated in Figure 3.1):

■ consulting, and

■ counselling

and synthesises these in his or her practice.

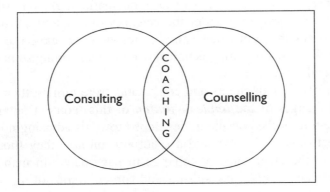

Figure 3.1 A marriage of two disciplines

Let us consider the two sources in turn.

Drawing on Consulting

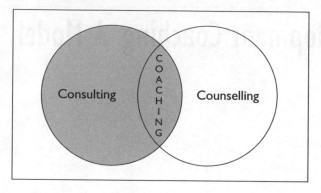

Content Consulting

Management consulting has a long history of its own, dating back to the beginning of the 20th century. In the 1980s, the 'strategy houses' (for example McKinsey, BCG, Bain & Co.) experienced explosive growth, not least of which came from the demand to respond to the phenomena described in the last chapter. The large consultancies that developed out of the original 'Big Eight' accountancy firms (for example as then, Andersen Consulting, Ernst & Young, Pricewaterhouse) also expanded into operational consulting and beyond, to offer strategic, technological and other specialist consulting (for example marketing, HR). All of these specialisms fell primarily under the category of 'content consulting'. A content consultant (sometimes called a 'resource' or 'expert' consultant) helps the client by providing technical expertise and doing something for, and on behalf of, the client.

By the 1990s, both clients and consultants were turning their attention to the challenges of the *implementation* of this 'content' advice. As a result, the role of the consultant developed towards advising not only on *what* client organisations should do, but also on *how* they should do it. This led to the emergence of 'change management', in many ways a fusion between content consulting and 'process consulting', an older tradition that stemmed from organisational development.

Process Consulting

According to a textbook on management consulting by Milan Kubr:

the [process] consultant as the agent of change attempts to help the organisation to solve its own problems by making it aware of organisational processes, of their likely consequences, and of intervention techniques for stimulating change. Instead of passing on technical knowledge and suggesting solutions, the process consultant is primarily concerned with passing on his approach, methods and values so that the client organisation itself can diagnose and remedy its own problems ... The process specialist focuses chiefly on the interpersonal and intergroup dynamics affecting the process of problem solving and change. He must bring all his role skills to bear on helping the client. He works on developing joint client–consultant diagnostic skills for addressing specific and relevant problems in order to focus on how things are done rather than on what tasks are performed.[1]

A New Blend of Content and Process

In her book, *Management Consultancy in the 21st Century*, Fiona Czerniawska quotes a BCG partner as saying: 'one of the most significant challenges facing consulting firms in the future will be the need to balance an empathetic process, which engages the client on an emotional level, with a high degree of analytical rigour – "content"'.[2]

Czerniawska also contends that:

in the 'ideal' consulting assignment, because of the strengths and weaknesses of each model, [content] and process-based consulting would occur together in an optimum ratio – an equilibrium of the two styles that is precisely tailored to the needs of the individual problem faced.[3]

We believe that what we have described as development coaching may be uniquely able to respond to this challenge by offering an individualised blend of content and process consulting.

Coach Laurence Lyons states the case for this blend's contribution to business strategy well:

In an era in which leadership is replacing management and learning is replacing instruction, coaching is surfacing as the accessible face of strategy. Business strategy no longer commands an exclusive domain secreted within the impersonal body of an abstract 'organisation'. Today, as demands on everyone's time intensify, strategy is manifest in the flesh and blood of each executive. Coaching is not simply a passing fad: it offers a pragmatic supporting context in which modern strategy flourishes. In today's turbulent world, strategy has developed into something that emerges, always tracking a moving target. And the preferred vehicle – responsive enough to reduce the risk in successfully travelling toward that ever-changing destination – is to be found in the dialogue of coaching.[4]

Thus, the development coach can effectively play the role of a 'personal management consultant', understanding both business/strategy and psychology/human behaviour in order to facilitate *content* improvement via *process* improvement.

Edgar Schein captures the complex and challenging nature of this blend well:

> If coaching is to be successful, the coach must be able, like a consultant, to create a helping relationship with his or her client. To create such a helping relationship, it is necessary to start in a process mode, which involves the learner/client, identifies the real problems, and builds a team in which both the coach and the client take responsibility for the outcomes. How the coaching relationship develops varies according to who initiated the process, the status differential between coach and client, whether the client is working on individual or organisational problems, and whether the context of the coaching concerns organisational mission and goals or organisational process and means. In each of these situations, the coach should have the ability to move easily among the roles of process consultant, content expert, and diagnostician/prescriber. The ultimate skill of the coach, then, is to assess the moment-to-moment reality that will enable him or her to be in the appropriate role.[5]

Although consulting and coaching are closely related, we believe there remain two key distinctions between them:

- One-to-one development coaching focuses on the *individual* as the means to facilitating organisational change

- Development coaching stops short of providing substantial content *advice*

Drawing on Counselling

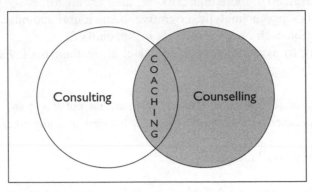

Essential Qualities

While consulting may provide valuable insights into both the content and process of a client's context, it is a coach's counselling ability that creates the conditions which enable the executive to reflect more deeply and personally upon the meaning he or she makes of this content and process. This can be a challenging experience, as described by Bennis:

> Learning from experience means looking back at your own childhood and adolescence and using what happened to you then to enable you to make things happen now, so that you become the master of your own life rather than its servant, consciously seeking the kinds of experiences in the present that will improve and enlarge you, taking risks as a matter of course, with the knowledge that failure is as vital as it is inevitable, seeing the future – yours and the world's – as an opportunity to do all those things you have not done and those things that need to be done, rather than as a trial or a test.[6]

In order to create a climate of safety and trust in which a client feels comfortable exploring such territory, a coach needs to bring to the relationship:

- acceptance of the client
- empathic understanding of his or her experiences
- congruence in providing honest feedback regarding his or her way of being

These are counselling qualities and skills.

Since the mid-1960s, the number of counselling and therapeutic models has grown from 60 to more than 250. Yet they are all still based upon three basic schools – psychoanalytic, cognitive–behavioural and humanistic. We briefly describe each of these schools in Appendix 2.

According to psychotherapists Miller et al. in their book *Escape from Babel*:

> forty years of sophisticated outcome research has not found any one theory, model or package of techniques to be reliably better than any other.[7]

However, they conclude that:

> there are few things in the field of psychology for which the evidence is so strong as that supporting the necessity, if not sufficiency, of the therapist conditions of accurate empathy, respect or warmth, and therapeutic genuineness.[8]

We briefly outline these three crucial counselling skills or qualities below:

- *Acceptance:* Acceptance is the fundamental *attitude* required by a counsellor or coach regarding the worth and significance of his or her client. Carl Rogers, a major founder of modern counselling, posed some challenging questions to test the genuineness of our attitude of acceptance:

> How do we look upon others? Do we see each person as having worth and dignity in his own right? If we do hold this point of view at the verbal level, to what extent is it operationally evident at the behavioural level? Do we tend to treat individuals as persons of worth, or do we subtly devaluate them by our attitudes and behaviour? Is our philosophy one in which respect for the individual is uppermost? Do we respect his capacity and his right to self-direction, or do we basically believe that his life could be best guided by us? To what extent do we have a need and a desire to dominate others? Are we willing for the individual to select and choose his own values, or are our actions guided by the conviction (usually unspoken) that he would be happiest if he permitted us to select for him his values and standards and goals?[9]

- *Empathic understanding:* This describes the fundamental *process* in counselling or coaching – outwardly manifested by verbal reflecting, summarising and questioning – that enables a client to hear him or herself accurately, as unfiltered by the coach's 'frame of reference' as possible. Rogers describes empathic understanding as a process in which:

the [counsellor] is sensing the feelings and personal meanings which the client is experiencing in each moment, when he can perceive these from 'inside', as they seem to the client, and when he can successfully communicate something of that understanding to his client.[10]

■ *Congruence:* If acceptance is an 'attitude' and empathic understanding is a 'process', congruence is a 'state of being'. Rogers describes the significance of congruence:

It has been found that personal change is facilitated when the [counsellor] is what he is, when in the relationship with his client he is genuine and without 'front' or façade, openly being the feelings and attitudes which at that moment are flowing in him ... The feelings the [counsellor] is experiencing are available to him, available to his awareness, and he is able to live these feelings, be them, and able to communicate them if appropriate.[11]

The congruent coach earns a client's trust by being a person who is willing to be fully present as a real, alive, relating human being. By being consistently congruent or authentic, the coach offers the client feedback on the effects which the client's behaviour has on another human being whose integrity can be trusted, and whose professionalism has ensured that, as far as possible, that reflection is not coloured by the coach's own needs.

There is, however, a crucial distinction between coaching and counselling. Counselling is a form of personal development that is most commonly sought by an individual to explore personal difficulties or issues, while coaching is intended primarily to address an individual's professional life and ultimately enable him or her to make a greater contribution to his or her organisation.

The Marriage: Development Coaching

So, if we have described each 'marriage partner' and its relationship to coaching, what constitutes the 'marriage'?

The marriage of consulting and counselling seems to represent a continuum, from most business oriented to most personal. As Figure 3.2 illustrates, this continuum has other characteristics implied by the nature of the orientation.

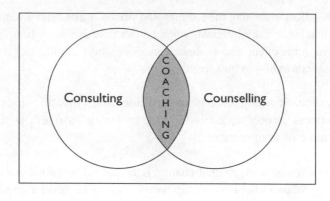

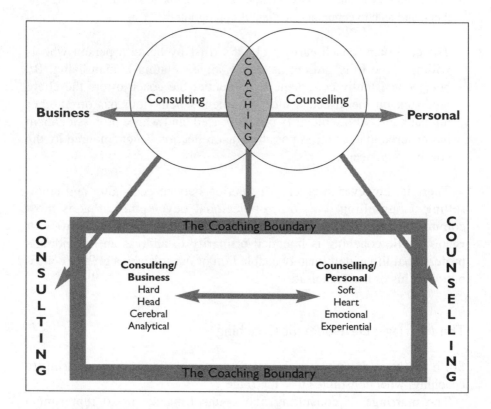

Figure 3.2 A business to personal continuum of coaching

The further right one goes on the continuum, the more private and sensitive the issues tend to be. Therefore, the development coach should only enter that territory a) out of necessity, that is, to achieve the client's goals, and b) with the client's permission.

However, a coach needs to be able to shift left or right along the continuum with ease, deploying the range of skills required to facilitate the client's learning in the most appropriate mode at that time. This process can shift between sessions or within minutes. For example, a coach and client might agree to devote one session to discussing the client's vision for his or her business (that is, ostensibly further left on the continuum) and the next session to an exploration of how and why he or she responds to confrontational situations with colleagues in a certain way (that is, further right). However, a more spontaneous shift might be required within the session discussing vision if the client starts to explore his or her personal values and desires for the business and him or herself.

The coach must therefore operate with a very wide and finely tuned 'radar screen', attending to a myriad of signals simultaneously and making very subtle choices regarding which signals to respond to. The coach's own process in doing this should be as transparent to the client as possible, continually engaging the client in a dialogue to select the most appropriate content to be discussed at any given time.

We described in Chapter 1 that a core activity in professional development coaching is creating the conditions for individual learning – experiencing, reflecting on the experience, theorising on what that experience means and then testing out that theory in practice. The coach encourages the client to stand back from the workplace and creates a dialogue in which the executive can gain perspective on his or her experiences and self, and on his or her leadership task within the organisation. And we have now described how, in creating this dialogue, the coach draws on a range of knowledge and experience, particularly from two disciplines: consulting and counselling. This enables a unique contribution of coaching to blend the 'hard' content and 'soft' process characterising those two disciplines. As this blending of content and process is key to an understanding of development coaching, let us explore it a little more in depth.

Making sense of subjective reality involves theorising. The human being is an active constructor of experience and may be seen as operating like a 'lay theorist'. We each build our understanding of reality around us (including that experienced in work) by interpreting the experience we have. That meaning-making is continually added to and refined in a continuous dynamic process of acting/doing, reflecting, theorising, acting/doing – just as represented in the Kolb learning cycle. Where the filters of

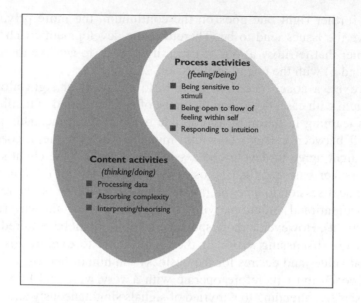

Figure 3.3 Blending content and process

our personal psychology are removed, that process will be functional and adaptive. But that adaptiveness depends on us being fully open not only to our cognitive, but equally important, to our affective (or emotional) experiencing – our '*being*'. The more thoughtfully we approach the business of living and leading and the more we remove the filters of habit and conditioned thinking and feeling, the more creative and unique will be our understanding and the self-expression we enact.

We believe that development coaching is unusual in seeking to hold content activities (thinking/doing) and process activities (feeling/being) together in parallel, as illustrated in Figure 3.3. As such, it can offer a powerful and pragmatic opportunity to individuals to learn to express themselves authentically and innovatively in their work (and life).

Professional Development Coaching: A Context for Nurturing Leadership

Understanding Leadership

We believe that one of the main drivers for the evolution of coaching is that it provides a context for individuals to explore their development needs as leaders. We suggest, therefore, that an important purpose of professional development coaching is *to assist those in leadership positions to develop the awareness, perspective, clarity of thought and emotional responsiveness to occupy their roles authentically and creatively.* Our case is that development coaching may be particularly relevant as a method for developing leadership because the processes involved in becoming an effective leader essentially call upon the ability to integrate content and process – doing and being.

Let us look at two writers on leadership to illustrate what we are saying. Alistair Mant in *Intelligent Leadership* undertakes an analysis of the processes of leadership and qualities of leaders.[12] His thesis is that successful leadership is a function of certain qualities of character and certain attributes of intelligence. He draws on Gardner's work on intelligence, which suggests that there may be seven forms of intelligence and that successful leaders show good functioning across the whole range of intelligences; they have versatility, or 'bandwidth'.[13]

Mant highlights the ability of 'broadbanders' to hold thinking and doing activities in parallel process – to mix thinking and doing together. (He refers to this as 'thinkering': oscillating between reflecting and testing out the product of that reflection.)

Mant also underscores the moral component in leadership. For leaders to be successful, they must be admired, and we admire them because they serve the task or common purpose of the organisation. They are intelligent, effective and are worth respecting because they are not self-serving. Mant implies that such people have a quality of 'authenticity' – those around them experience them as 'real'.

Warren Bennis comments at length on this quality of authenticity in his book on American leaders, *On Becoming a Leader*. He regards successful leadership, fundamentally, as a function of being personally authentic. That process is an evolutionary one and comes out of increased self-awareness through reflection:

> Reflecting on experience is a means of having a Socratic dialogue with yourself, asking the right questions at the right time, in order to discover the truth of yourself and your life. What really happened? Why did it happen? What did it do to me? What did it mean to me? In this way, one locates and appropriates the knowledge one needs or, more precisely, recovers what one knew but had forgotten, and becomes, in Goethe's phrase, the hammer rather than the anvil.[14]

Such self-awareness involves untying oneself from one's past, received view of the world:

we have the means within us to free ourselves from the constraints of the past which lock us into imposed roles and attitudes. By examining and understanding the past, we can move into the future unencumbered by it, *we become free to express ourselves, rather than endlessly trying to prove ourselves.*[15]

The active and evolved part of self-awareness, then, is self-expression and that self-expression is developed through thinking innovatively and autonomously in the process of interacting with others within the context of one's own working life.

There is considerable overlap in what Bennis and Mant are saying. Both see leadership as an active, engaged, intelligent and self-directing mode of being in work. 'Leadership is first being, then doing. Everything the leader does reflects what he or she is.'[16] Mant acknowledges that, with a background in childhood which was truly nurturing, any of us could fully function in the terms he describes, and Bennis sees the process of becoming a leader as 'much the same as the process of becoming an integrated human being. For the leader, as for any integrated person, life itself is the career.'[17] In the case studies analysed by both writers, we see examples of innovative, self-expressing behaviour, as well as an extraordinary ability to absorb complexity and understand and give it shape. These behaviours and attributes, we believe, may be developed.

To summarise, successful, creative leadership is in part a function of being in the service of a common group or organisational purpose. Within that context, the better able the individual is to operate intelligently and authentically (experimentally and undefensively), the more likely he or she will be able to give shape and direction to his or her enterprise or part of it – offering a leadership which is relevant and respected. Natural endowment or psychological inflexibility may limit the level of organisational and conceptual complexity in which an individual may successfully manage and offer leadership. But, by committing to a process of self-awareness through learning, opening to experience (both internal and external) and experimentation, any leader prepared to take the risk of this way of being in work will gain considerably greater competence and inner authority.

Professional Coaching for Leadership Development

What, then, are the core activities involved in development coaching with the particular aim of developing leadership of the kind we describe? We believe these to be twofold:

■ To assist the individual leader to develop greater 'bandwidth' – to think and act with greater versatility

■ To assist him or her to develop authenticity – to become open to the whole of his or her experiencing

With a focus on the leadership role, coaching will pay particular attention to enabling the client leader to:

■ reflect on current experience: forming theories about the context in which he or she exercises leadership and about his or her role within that context

■ articulate his or her understanding of the organisation (its environment and the organisational and interpersonal dynamics at play) and test his or her internal response against the connections or insights so articulated

■ become open and sensitised to the play of his or her emotions and intuition in response to the events he or she is experiencing

■ 'thinker' (to use Mant's expression): move towards an experimental mode in which action and thought are held in parallel process, in the light of the 'theory' that the individual has developed about the particular interaction/event/organisational analysis/strategy in question

We believe that, at all levels of leadership, the central processes of development coaching will remain the same, as outlined in the bullet points above. In the case of chief executives of large organisations, however, the coach may well need to demonstrate personal credibility as a collaborator at this level, as well as particular sector experience. But these qualifications are likely to have more to do with meeting the chief executive's preconditions for engaging in coaching than representing a different coaching approach.

Summary

In this chapter, we have shown how professional development coaching draws on the disciplines of consulting and counselling, blending them to create a discipline in its own right. Our case is that development coaching not only provides a highly appropriate context for addressing the development needs of those in senior positions within organisations, but that it also provides a particularly useful, and possibly unique, means for those in these positions to develop competency in creative, responsive leadership and to articulate their own authentic leadership style.

In the next chapter, we illustrate development coaching with three senior executives, each confronted with a different leadership challenge.

Notes

1. M. Kubr (ed.) *Management Consulting: A Guide to the Profession,* 2nd edn (Geneva: International Labour Office, 1986) pp. 44, 48.
2. F. Czerniawska, *Management Consultancy in the 21st Century* (London: Macmillan Business – now Palgrave, 1999) p. 141.
3. Ibid., p. 114.
4. L. Lyons, 'Coaching at the Heart of Strategy', in M. Goldsmith (ed.) *Coaching for Leadership: How the World's Greatest Coaches Help Leaders Learn* (San Francisco: Jossey-Bass, 2000) pp. 10–11.
5. E. Schein, 'Coaching and Consultancy', in M. Goldsmith (ed.) *Coaching for Leadership: How the World's Greatest Coaches Help Leaders Learn* (San Francisco: Jossey-Bass, 2000) p. 72.
6. W. Bennis, *On Becoming a Leader* (Reading, MA: Perseus Books, 1994) pp. 99–100.
7. S.D. Miller, B.L. Duncan and M.A. Hubble (eds), *Escape from Babel: Toward a Unifying Language for Psychotherapy Practice* (New York: W.W. Norton & Company, 1997) p. 2.
8. Ibid., p. 84.
9. C. Rogers, *Client-Centred Therapy* (London: Constable, 1951) p. 20.
10. C. Rogers, *On Becoming a Person* (Boston: Houghton Mifflin, 1961) p. 62.
11. Ibid., p. 61.
12. A. Mant, *Intelligent Leadership* (New South Wales, Australia: Allen & Unwin, 1997).
13. H. Gardner, *Frames of Mind, The Theory of Multiple Intelligences* (New York: Basic Books, 1993).
14. W. Bennis, *On Becoming a Leader* (Reading, MA: Perseus Books, 1994) p. 61.
15. Ibid., p. 79.
16. Ibid., p. 141.
17. Ibid., p. 4.

CHAPTER 4

Case Studies

Introduction

The aim of this chapter is to give a flavour of the subtlety and impact of professional coaching for leadership development in practice. We take three of our actual client cases to illustrate three different points of departure in enhancing leadership performance:

- developing leadership at a senior level for the first time
- recovering leadership impetus
- refocusing existing, competent leadership

This is the 'what' of the work. At the same time, we seek to illustrate different ways in which content and process (cognitive and emotional connecting: doing and being) may be blended. This is the 'how' of the coaching to be described in Chapter 5.

The case studies are anonymous in order to maintain the confidentiality of those concerned. These are, however, actual cases and each person involved has reviewed what is written here and comments on his or her own experience of the coaching a year or so on.

Case Study 4.1

Leadership Revealed

Background

Sheila Davis is a board director. She has been with her organisation for ten years and a year ago was promoted to her present position. In an executive board of ten, she was one of three women but the only woman in operations.

Emerging Issues

I was invited by the human resources department to meet with Sheila. At our meeting, Sheila outlined the situation openly and directly. She described the Board as very competitive. The culture was male and macho, but trying to change. She felt quite paralysed on the Board and when she was paralysed she could not think. The second issue was her relationship with her boss. He was a powerful and somewhat feared, long-standing senior member of the company. She had little sense of how she was doing in his eyes and was concerned that she might be underperforming. She was feeling under pressure and vulnerable within the organisation. She wanted, therefore, to build a relationship with her boss, to define her contribution to the Board and to develop a method of supporting herself.

We agreed to work together for a year and that we would start by reviewing in depth her background, career and current situation which would then provide a clearer focus for our work. The objectives that emerged in that review fell into three areas:

1. developing a belief in herself

2. developing skills in managing her own state and her relationship to others

3. learning to contribute to changing the organisation's culture

from which we produced a more detailed contract against which we subsequently monitored the progress of the coaching.

Working on the Agenda

Sheila and I worked quite organically on these issues. That is to say, we would take a particular issue or a particular situation and use it to work freely, in an unstructured way, on the objectives agreed in the contract. The commentary below seeks to illustrate the work we did on some of these.

Work on Her Belief in Herself

At the outset, we both noticed that Sheila needed plenty of support for her sense of herself, which she tended to lose when she felt isolated. We noticed, also, that unless she was part of what was happening she felt on the outside. When she felt this way, she allowed herself to become marginalised. Self-support meant that she needed to engage rather than stand on the sidelines, but engagement meant different things in different situations. We agreed that the task was to develop connected relationships with other people, starting with the members of her team of peers. Her aim should be to develop strong one-to-one relationships with the people concerned, as a means of becoming comfortable with herself in that group. Within three or four sessions of working with Sheila on selected key relationships, she began to blossom in confidence. I noticed how she was now moving towards the people concerned and being open with them, and how well this was working in getting feedback from others that they liked what they saw when she did this. Her confidence in herself as a member of the group grew as a consequence. Four months later, she became clearer that being involved, valuing her femaleness and intuition and being prepared to stand up for what her guts told her when she was in tune with them, served her in good stead. She continued to go towards people and confirmed that the number of people with whom she could be open was increasing.

By the end of the process, her performance review with her boss indicated that there had been a great improvement and that she had contributed substantially to creating high performance from her team. When we analysed the situation, we saw that Sheila had developed considerable moral authority both within the team and as an individual. She had a strong sense of principle and had now developed the confidence in herself to represent principle within the team.

Managing the Relationship with Her Boss

We devoted a whole one-and-a-half-hour session to this relationship. I invited her beforehand to complete a questionnaire on her boss which asked her to describe his background, objectives, motivations, what he valued and what he was threatened by, and so on. Sheila took us through her answers and I reflected back to her the sense of the person I had picked up from her, and from this we together created a picture of him as a person. We spent some time investigating this and became clear that it was of central importance to him to be seen as someone who delivered results and that he be in a position to manage expectations around him in order to achieve this successfully. Nothing seemed to frighten him, but he disliked lack of knowledge, clarity and direction in others. So we agreed that Sheila should take charge of their relationship and give him early warning of proposals or problems so that he could absorb these and manage others' expectations accordingly. We then came up with an action plan. She should set up regular meetings at monthly intervals with her boss, which would be programmed at the beginning of the day when time was more under control. She should set up an initial meeting to explain the purpose of these regular meetings and get his agreement to it. She should chair the meeting and organise it around the following structure:

■ Report on progress on key projects

■ Address key issues where she needed his input on work in her area

■ Periodically review with him how well their meetings were working from each others' point of view

At our next meeting, which was five weeks later, Sheila reported that she had now instituted these meetings. She had taken charge of the meeting and her boss acknowledged this and pronounced himself happy with the way it was working. She noticed, however, that she had a tendency to default to being the 'angry child' with him. I ran through the transactional analysis Parent/Adult/Child model on a flip chart briefly, and she understood immediately the process I was describing. I suggested to her that her task with her boss was to stay in 'adult mode' with him and that, when he became 'parental' (which he tended to do when frustrated), she should find ways of supporting herself and avoiding getting hooked. She should see her task as one of managing him upwards and to do that, she had to stay well centred and understand that the behaviour she was seeing was a function of his personality rather than of her behaviour.

This awareness served her well and it helped her in maintaining an adult relationship with him, which he then responded well to, and it undoubtedly contributed to the good level of collaboration that they had achieved by the end of the year. (On a number of occasions, I used simple models such as Parent/Adult/Child, and it was interesting to notice how Sheila was able to use these on the basis of understanding intuitively what was being said and apply them pragmatically and effectively.)

Contributing to the Organisation

At the halfway point in our work, I invited Sheila to review who was in the company at her level and above, with whom she needed to build collaborative relationships and sponsorship if she was to be effective in contributing to the change in culture in the organisation. From this, she developed a plan of action to develop her relationships with identified board members and an important colleague who could block her in another department. By deliberately making herself more visible and taking the initiative in this respect, she moved towards them and connected. Once she connected personally, then her openness, directness and intelligence worked well for her and she got the recognition and respect that she needed.

As a result of that interaction and thinking about it, she became clear about the need for her to develop greater clarity in strategic thinking. Strategic thinking meant to her contributing to the corporate debate as it occurred in the moment, from meeting to meeting. She was fine working offline, but wanted to respond with bright ideas in the way that she saw other directors doing. By examining a recent group meeting, we came to recognise that she had good capacity to develop ideas in other settings. It was rather that she felt inhibited when she saw herself as existing on the margin of the group. She came to recognise that being effective at senior level meant developing the capacity to flex successfully between varying roles, using different strengths in different settings as the situation demanded, and putting in place the conditions for one's own successful performance. She then realised that the best contribution she could make was to challenge thinking rather than to compete over its articulation. Subsequently, she shifted her stance in the light of this understanding and gained substantial recognition both from her peers and her boss of her contribution to the better functioning of the groups of which she was a member. She showed particular leadership in developing relationships with suppliers and developing collaboration between them and the company on the basis of acting upon her values of inclusiveness, directness and openness. Indeed, a year later, she was described by the chief executive as the person within the company who was contributing most to changing the organisation's culture and was given a change in role which made this leadership visible throughout the company.

Our Process

We worked by looking at the particular. If Sheila felt that she had lost ground in a meeting of her team, for example, then I asked her to describe in detail what had happened. In particular, I would ask her what she was feeling or had felt as the process went on. I would then reflect to her what I had heard and offer some connections that occurred to me both from what she had said in the past and what she was saying now. Between us, we would build up a 'theory' of what was happening. The process of learning took place in building personal insights. The building of her self-awareness through collaborative theorising based on reflecting her to herself was exciting. She said she looked forward to our sessions and felt excited in anticipation; I did too. By listening carefully to the material, particularly emotional material, I opened up for her what she was feeling behind any defensive reaction, and we devised ways of responding on the basis of those feelings and her sense of herself. She would then apply this and we would review the success of what she had done when we next met. Sometimes, we would stand right back and I would remind her of her values and of her positive sense of herself, in order to counter the harsh reaction she continued to show towards herself. At another time in the same session, or even the same discussion, we focused right down into a practical piece of action, for example how she might prepare for an important meeting.

Conclusion

At the end of our work, I invited Sheila to describe what she had learned and wished to take away from our year together. In our final session, she summarised what she had learned:

- She had developed a strength of belief in herself – in 'being me'

- She had learned to manage her emotional state and to keep herself in a more positive mindset

- She had got better at confronting, managing upwards and acting on her own instinct

- She had learned that developing effective one-to-one relationships was for her a powerful means of engaging with a team and moving its behaviour

■ She had learned the importance of persistence – being confident in her beliefs and in herself helped her to keep going

■ She had discovered that taking a stand works

She said that what had been particularly helpful was me giving her feedback on what I was hearing her saying. She had also found it helpful when I was able to feed perceptions of people back to her in a way that helped her to see them, not as people with two heads, but ordinary people. She liked the format of our work – she worked and I reflected the substance of that work, her thinking and feelings, back to her. She liked being given 'homework' (experimenting with new behaviour) and the gap between sessions allowed her to practise. She liked the way I was able to join thinking and feeling together for her. She also liked the fact that we were practical and dealt with some straightforward issues, the understanding from which then carried over into other areas. Finally, that she kept taking from me the comment 'I notice that …'. She kept on noticing her own behaviour and managing it better as a result of that self-awareness. As a result of our work, she had now come to appreciate that she had skills that were valuable and were valued and learned a lightness of touch, which had served her well.

Postscript: Sheila Davis

I have asked Sheila to comment on this process 18 months after it was completed. Here are her remarks:

> Our work on building one-to-one relationships with the other team members as a means of being effective within the group as a whole was a key part of the coaching process for me. Eighteen months on, working with a new team of people, I find myself comfortable with myself, but not with the new team members as yet. However, I recognise my process from the first time round and find that learning from the previous experience is helping me adapt much faster than before.

> What is striking for me is that the relationship with my boss is now so radically different. At the beginning of coaching, our relationship was one in which I looked up to him and sought his advice. Now, my boss often seeks my advice and support.

> A key part of the coaching process for me was the linking of feeling with thinking. I learned to use my feelings and trust them, and this has helped me to take my place in the team, and with top management, with confidence in what was for me earlier, a rather threatening male, analytic culture, where my emotional responsiveness (and that of others) seemed to be undervalued and dismissed.

> The coaching process has worked very well for me.

Case Study 4.2

Leadership Asserted

Background

Alistair Leith was finance director of a £150 million-turnover manufacturing business. He had been in this position for about ten years, number two in the organisation to two successive CEOs. Prior to joining the company he had held a number of senior positions in multinationals and blue-chip management consultancies.

Emerging Issues

At our first meeting, Alistair ran over his career in the company. He had been head-hunted into his current post ten years ago. During those ten years a number of exciting developments had taken place, which he offered initially as a reason for not having moved on. However, he later acknowledged that he was someone who, while confident in his own core competencies, was not confident about taking on new responsibilities, and was risk averse with regard to his own career. Now 50, he recognised that he was not stretching himself and was concerned that he might become stale in the job. He was therefore looking for an opportunity to review his thinking about his current situation and future career.

What emerged was a picture of paralysis. Alistair was a person who in some ways had not realised his full potential. He had succeeded beyond his wildest dream in achieving a position of status, but now felt that he had not become all that he might. He had another ten years to go, and wanted to become a CEO, but doubted that it would now be easy for him to find such a post at another company.

The picture of paralysis extended to the Board. The company was in a 'Cinderella sector' and needed greater scale. It was undervalued by the stock market in spite of having performed very well in recent years. It had expanded as far as it could do, given a depressed share price. The Board, largely made up of non-executive directors, needed urgently to work out a strategy for the longer term, but seemed unable to address this.

We both felt that Alistair's best opportunity to develop his role lay within the company, and agreed that the coaching contract should therefore comprise the following agenda:

- Develop his thinking on the future strategy for the company
- Review his role in the light of that thinking and opportunities for enhancing it
- Address those issues that had been holding him back from being proactive in his own interest

Working on the Agenda

Our work together over the next 12 months went through four stages. The first was relatively short, the task being to facilitate Alistair in developing his own thinking on the future strategy for the company. As we did this, he reached the conclusion that the major asset in the company was its executive management team. It had the ability to manage a more sophisticated operation. He was enthusiastic to build the strategic capacity of that team and to lead it. What emerged then was clarity that the company needed either to be bought out by the management team or be acquired by (reversing into) a larger competitor, forming a significant combined presence. In either scenario, he and his chief executive needed to work closely together, with a common view of that strategy. While they worked reasonably effectively together, the relationship was not a close one.

The second stage, therefore, was to build a closer relationship with the chief executive founded on a good level of trust between them. Alistair realised that it would be for him to move the relationship forward, but was at a loss as to how to do this. We spent time considering the make-up and the motivation of his CEO and constructed together the nature of an opening dialogue with him. This proved successful and quickly strengthened the collaboration between the two men. From that came a clear indication from his CEO – who proposed to step down once the strategy of Management Buy-out (MBO) or being acquired had been successfully achieved – that he would sponsor Alistair as the next CEO of the company.

The third stage involved Alistair taking a leading role in confronting the Board with the realities facing it, and then, with the Board's permission, exploring with advisors the viability of a MBO, while in parallel initiating exploratory meetings with potential purchasers. He gained confidence and credibility in this process, and, with his CEO's support, came to be seen as the key player by potential purchasers. As discussions matured and the value placed on the business by the potential purchasers increased, Alistair formed the view that being acquired offered the most exciting and creative future for the management team. This development happened within three months and the company was bought due to the value the acquiring European parent felt it could add to the new group's strategic development and positioning.

Stage four took place during the last four months of the coaching contract. The focus of our work was now on understanding the new Pan-European organisation, identifying the required strategy for the group and the role that he and his team sought to play in this. Alistair became keen to have an option on becoming CEO of the whole company, a post that was likely to become available within the next two years.

Our Process

The main way in which Alistair used me was as a sounding board. He prepared carefully for our meetings and would take me through developments and through his thinking. Thinking might be about board strategy or about a particular management issue that was inhibiting the progress of that strategy. I would summarise and reflect what I was hearing, as well as any dissonance I noticed between the intentions I heard him articulate and his behaviour as he reported it to me or as I experienced it in our sessions. He took notes of our meetings and reported that he kept these at hand when he moved around the company. When we had completed our first year's work, Alistair took out an eight-hour retainer for he wished to continue to have the opportunity to test his thinking outside the company.

Generally speaking, we worked at the cognitive end of the coaching continuum (as described in Chapter 3), focusing on his business issues. But we did not do this exclusively. We had noted at the outset that Alistair was quite risk averse with regard to his career. When we examined the rational basis to this risk aversion, he came to realise that his personal financial platform was in place and that any action he took need not put this in jeopardy. The impact was striking. He said later that the single most important insight he had got from our work was that he could afford to be entrepreneurial with his career, and was staggered, he said, that it had not become obvious to him before.

I also encouraged him to become more open and direct. My experience of him in the early stage of our relationship was that he was careful in revealing himself and I felt that his ability to lead others might be inhibited by this 'closedness' (for it might be difficult for others to read him). In particular, I encouraged him to be direct with his CEO about his wishes and feelings in the discussions described above. The impact of his doing this was noticeable. He commented on how much more incisive he had become within the first three months of our work together, and felt this was because his self-confidence had increased as he risked being more open. These shifts in themselves were quite minor, but the results were dramatic, as he 'got off the fence', and committed himself. He had always had great competence – 'a good hand of cards' – and now he had the confidence to play it.

Conclusion

Coaching had been useful to Alistair in providing him with the opportunity to articulate his thinking and his doubts, and particularly because of the confidential nature of the setting, to acknowledge what was inhibiting him. I believe that my ability to reflect to him accurately both his thinking and his doubts, as well as the gentle challenge that our work offered to him to live more fully, gave him sufficient support to tip the balance quite significantly towards taking the steps he did. In the early stages, my encouragement to identify the action he would take and report back on it was, I believe, helpful in getting the ball rolling with a process that then began to move well by itself.

During our work, Alistair stressed on a number of occasions how useful coaching had been. In the early stages, he fed back to me his chief executive's approving comments about how much more positive he was becoming. He also fed back to me on several occasions how helpful talking through particular management problems had proved and, on one occasion, he expressed the view that our work had for him been truly 'developmental'. My feeling was that coaching had provided the setting and impetus for change that was very ready to happen within him.

Alistair had set out to look at his career, consider the opportunities within his current setting and address what might be inhibiting him from grasping these. Those objectives were achieved quite dramatically. His team had grown in capacity and were a leading force within the new combined company, and, as a team, they were producing by far the best performance of the new group. Alistair himself was clearly a credible contender for the position of group CEO, when this became available.

One final point of interest is that although Alistair had felt coaching had been helpful to him, and although on a number of occasions he had raised the possibility of coaching for his direct reports, this never materialised. At the end, I reviewed this with him and he acknowledged that when he became chief executive he felt reluctant to share his coach with others. We believe this is a common reaction of CEOs and one that should be borne in mind by any coaching organisation anticipating a cascade of work from coaching at the top of an organisation.

Postscript: Alistair Leith

Even before the coaching process began, I was convinced I was capable of achieving much more in my career. I had considered extended formal training (at Harvard or Insead), but I thought a one-to-one assessment of where I was going would be more productive.

In the early stages, I was very conscious of a methodology being employed. Indeed, the process was explained at the outset in terms of objectives, milestones and deliverables, all in a planned sequence. Nevertheless, I feel what Mike has written above fairly reflects my own experience of what happened. As the months passed and Mike and I got used to each other, our conversations and debates seemed natural, so much so that I started to consider him to be an important extension of my management team. In fact, I took out a retainer with Mike after we had met our original coaching objectives so that I could continue to use his input on the management issues facing me in the new job.

During the coaching contract we talked at length about personal security. As Mike says, the impact of this discussion was striking, and it was the realisation above anything else that I could afford to take more professional risk that helped me move forward quickly.

An unexpected benefit I have gained from coaching is that it has modelled for me a new way of working with my direct reports. I find myself in many conversations playing back to the individual concerned what I am hearing him say, and notice how useful it is as a means of helping him think things out.

Finally, the key point of coaching is that you must be open to change and ready to act on what you have learnt; the coach cannot do it for you; he can only make you more aware. Mutual trust is essential.

Case Study 4.3
Leadership Released

Background

Garry Parsons was the technical director of a high-tech chemical company, which had grown from scratch over 11 years to become a highly rated public company turning over £15 million and employing 200 people. Garry had been with the company from the beginning – one of initially three employees, having joined straight from completing his PhD at the age of 26.

Emerging Issues

At our first meeting, Garry described himself as 'just a scientist' until five years ago. Then the company was turning over only £200K, employing 15 people and still making a loss. At that point, Garry was head of chemistry. Collaboration with a large international company to develop transfer technology had led to spectacular growth. Now, he had suddenly become 'a big man in the company'. He was feeling somewhat out of his depth in the business in the face of the rapid growth of the company.

What he wanted was to consolidate his learning and build a platform of experience, confidence and competence as a manager and as a board director of a plc. He 'easily felt stupid on the Board' and, when he reported as a director, he tended to do so only in the safe area of technical matters rather than speaking to the issues confronting the Board. His job had been his life so far, and he felt unemployable outside the company for his experience was so limited. So he wanted to move away from being a specialist to developing his competence in general management.

We agreed the following agenda for our year's work:

1. To develop his skills as an operational director – particularly in respect of leading those reporting to him

2. To scope the competencies he required for future management and to plan how to develop these in his current role

3. To understand his role on the Board, develop his contribution as a board member and his confidence in that capacity

I noted how highly motivated I found him and expected that he would learn very fast. He wanted to work on practical problems that faced him in the job and coaching seemed an ideal medium for him to acquire the development he was seeking.

Working on the Agenda

Developing Performance as an Operational Director

We started by undertaking an analysis of the two key people reporting to Garry. From this, we identified the potential he believed they had and the areas in which they needed to develop. We brainstormed what their departments might look like in, say, two year's time given the rate of growth of the company and came up with an outline job specification. We then looked at the areas of development required in each case and finally considered how to gain the individuals' willing acceptance and commitment to what was being offered. In the case of one person, this meant confronting him very directly with his dismissive attitude towards working in teams.

We then looked at how he might develop his team of middle managers. They seemed in awe of him and tended to wait for his direction. We developed the idea for him to reinforce their accountability and autonomy by setting them up as a mini board with him as their non-executive chairman. He understood the idea immediately and, once again, applied it very quickly and with very good effect.

At the end of this phase of our work, I noted that Garry was a delight to work with because he picked up the learning so fast. I was to discover that he applied that learning equally fast. I noted also how he had found it difficult to confront issues of personal performance with the managers reporting to him, but quickly did so when he understood how to go about this and the need for doing so.

Garry, together with his CEO, was concerned about the performance of a fellow director who was responsible for the research side of the business and we examined the basis for this concern in some detail. He was able to offer good evidence to support his reservation and together we worked out how he might best act in the interests of the company. He followed through the plan we developed and expressed his concern professionally at the executive team meeting and in separate meetings with the CEO and then the director concerned. It was subsequently agreed that Garry should take over responsibility for running both the production and research sides of the business. This happened quite speedily and was done very well, with the fellow director taking on a science liaison role with major customers.

Garry's confidence grew in his ability to confront people effectively. His confidence was further increased by his success in taking over responsibility for research. He had got hold of the situation within a few weeks and the staff concerned expressed their confidence in him and his approach. The people he had been developing under him as a result of our earlier discussions were growing well and he was coming to realise that his own management and leadership style were stronger than he had thought.

Scoping Leadership at the Top

Within two months of Garry taking responsibility for both production and research across the company, his boss, the CEO, announced to the Board that he wished to leave the company within two years and was concerned about succession. He shared his view of Garry's potential with his fellow directors, and it was agreed that, while there could be no question of promising him the CEO position, Garry was the natural internal candidate and should be groomed for this.

The first step was to appoint him chief operating officer (COO). Garry was excited about this. Because those reporting to him were performing well, he was confident in taking on the responsibility. He quickly took the opportunity to formalise all project and management processes across the company, bringing increased discipline and rigour to them. He had by now discovered that he could operate well outside the framework of his own technical background in the company.

We now moved the focus of our work to identifying the areas where he needed development in the new role and beyond it, to strengthen his qualifications for becoming CEO. These included outlining in some detail the business plan for the next three years, and the structure and the management development needs of the organisation this implied. We also reviewed the working relationship he wished to develop with his colleagues on the executive team as he took charge of it.

Nine months after we had started work Garry had his first appraisal in the role of COO. His CEO commented:

> Consistency in dealing with people is one of the major skills he has already demonstrated as COO. Garry Parsons is most certainly viewed as a key leader within the company and it is the intention for this to be built upon in the future.

Working with the Board

Garry had initially felt in some awe of the non-executive directors on the Board. On several occasions, we talked about the issues they raised at board meetings and helped him express his own thinking about these. As his self-confidence in himself as an executive grew, and as he saw the contribution of the non-executive directors in better perspective, he felt able to express his opinions at board meetings. Quite quickly, he took a full part in board discussions. Two months after he became COO, he confronted the non-executive directors forthrightly on their indecisiveness over selling the company.

Our Process

The work with Garry was mainly at the cognitive end of the coaching continuum. I noted early that I found him to be an intelligent, highly motivated and well-integrated person. In fact, as we worked together, I noticed that as he revealed more of himself, he became more relaxed with me and I felt that I should give him more permission to express self-doubt than I had done, for I had been so impressed with him. This had the effect of allowing him to express where he doubted himself, and me to encourage him to discount this self-doubt, trust his intuition, and give himself permission to do things the way he felt he wanted to. I believe it was something of a relief to find out that it was all right for him to be himself and trust his own judgement. So, he used our work to test his thinking, and thus to increase his confidence that what he had in mind all along made sense. He then quickly implemented his plans and moved forward with great decisiveness.

At the end of the year of working together, I was struck with how far his self-perception had shifted.

Conclusion

In our final session, we reviewed what Garry valued from our work together:

- He handled people better now – both at board level and within the rest of the company

- He had learned a great deal about the development of managers and succession planning through our work

- He had developed his confidence with regards to the Board. He no longer doubted his right to be there and he felt comfortable with others being specialist in their area, leaving him to be a specialist in his

- Using me as a sounding board. It had been very useful to set out his own thinking and to hear different approaches that he would not have thought of. He noted how much he had learnt about confronting things more readily; he now did this routinely

He had appreciated our informal style of working. He liked the fact that we took particular issues that were current in themselves and, from the analysis of these, built up an understanding, from which he then generalised. For him, doing things in this bite-sized way had worked very well.

At the end of our contract I kept in touch with Garry and learned that within two months his CEO stood down and Garry was invited by the Board to take his place – 18 months before he had anticipated. He accepted the role with a will and felt that the challenge was an exciting one. While it had happened for the wrong reasons, it was an opportunity he relished.

Postscript: Garry Parsons

Working with my coach has radically altered my management and interaction at all levels within the company.

We began by looking at approaches to solving real, operational issues and how to manage my direct reports to best effect and gain buy-in from them to particular ideas/solutions I had in mind. This then expanded naturally to developing effective working relationships with my peer group, leadership of the team and finally leadership within the Board. The result for the company is a highly motivated, consistently managed workforce, and an executive management team that works as a real 'team' but has true leadership at all times. My confidence with the Board increased dramatically, and, whereas before I only felt competent technically, I now feel confident in my understanding and knowledge in the company's business, its markets and its technologies, and able to represent my views there strongly and effectively.

Mike easily identified how I thought and expressed myself and then worked in my language. Most importantly, he was able to establish a rapport with me that put me at my ease and created the safety to 'get it all out'. He noticed the issues behind the accounts of myself at work, and focused these accurately. He teased out the sense from my 'garbled intelligence' (as my school teachers used to describe it!) and recognised that I needed to put all the facts of an issue on the table before I could become clear about what to do. He read the situations I described accurately, identified the key issues for me, and where it called for it, worked with me to help resolve any underlying concern which might be blocking me.

Personally, working with my coach has taken away many of the stresses of being in a senior executive role, and I feel increased confidence in my ability to deal with stressful situations, and this, in particular, has benefited my home life and family enjoyment.

CHAPTER 5

The Process of Professional Development Coaching

In the last chapter, we provided snapshots of our development coaching work in the form of selected case studies. In this chapter, we aim to place these snapshots in a wider context by describing the underlying 'macro process' employed to provide structure and rigour in our work with clients (as distinct from the 'micro process' within each coaching session). In particular, this macro process is intended to support the purposive nature of development coaching described in Chapter 3 and to permit demonstration of both an individual and organisational benefit from the investment by the organisation.

We hope that our description will paint a picture for readers who may be considering development coaching for themselves or for colleagues, as well as provide a model for current or aspiring coaches to consider for their own practice. As we describe our model, we are aware of the difficult balance between providing enough detail to delineate the process without sounding too prescriptive.

The process typically lasts 12 months and falls into four broad, overlapping stages, as follows:

1. Contracting and relationship management

2. The work

3. Ongoing review and evaluation

4. Ending and managing feedback to the organisation

Contracting and Relationship Management

The platform for the process is a 'triangular contract' between the organisation, the coach and the client, against which everyone may monitor progress. If the client is self-sponsored, then the contract is simplified to a two-way contract between the client and coach. The guidelines below offer a means of maintaining this triangular contract with the parties involved:

- describe the coaching process

- define roles (for example coach, client, sponsor)

- engage sponsor and client commitment

- be explicit in how organisational and individual interests are to be balanced

- establish clear, mutual expectations

- identify realistic objectives and outcomes

- monitor and evaluate results with all stakeholders

Marketing Representation and Initial Communication with Sponsors

Ideally, contracting begins with the first communication that a professional development coach has with a prospective client and/or his or her organisation. The triangular relationship typically may then develop in the following order:

1. Prospective organisational sponsor and coach meet and agree that the coaching service on offer would help to achieve the organisation's objectives

2. Sponsor identifies potential client and briefs the coach

3. The coach arranges to meet the potential client for an exploratory meeting

During the initial meeting with the organisational sponsor, the coach might seek to establish the triangular contracting process by making explicit:

■ The coach's expectation that the sponsor will communicate openly to the client why he or she has been referred for coaching (including sharing the brief to the coach with the client)

■ All coaching programmes will have a written contract which will be shared between coach, client and sponsor

■ Progress against the contract will be formally evaluated halfway through the programme and at the end

In reality, referral to coaching tends to be more ad hoc. The organisation often does not have a clear understanding of what coaching is, or its application, until it has had some experience of it. In our experience, it may take up to a year of informal discussion with an organisation to reach the point of first referral. Nevertheless, it is useful to keep these guidelines in mind, and introduce them when it is timely to do so.

Exploratory Meeting Between Prospective Client and Coach

It is common practice for a coach to offer an initial, 'no commitment' exploratory meeting to a prospective client in order that he or she may have the opportunity to see if the chemistry feels right, learn how the coach practises and identify if the fit is right between what the coach can offer and what the client seeks.

At this meeting, the agenda that might be covered includes:

■ The client's current situation

■ His or her development needs and understanding/expectations of coaching

■ His or her perception of the organisation's expectations of the potential coaching

■ The coach's philosophy of development coaching (for example commitment to balancing the individual and organisational interests, to the contracting process and to accountability to mutually agreed upon measures of success) and way of working (for example the main elements of the process which this chapter is describing)

■ How the client may prefer to work in addressing his or her individual development needs in the light of his or her particular learning style

By the end of the meeting, the client and coach should feel clear about whether they are sufficiently comfortable with each other and with the potential agenda for working together.

Review Meeting and Contract Defining

If the client wishes to proceed, the development coaching programme usually begins with a review meeting, the objectives of which may include:

1. To facilitate the client in taking stock of the key elements of his or her self and leadership, especially understanding the formative influences throughout his or her life

2. To allow the coach and client to understand the client in some depth, and to begin to build the relationship

3. To identify the key issues and development needs the client wishes to address, which will form the basis of the coaching contract

4. To draft a coaching contract with clear measures of success by which all stakeholders will be able to monitor progress and results

The review meeting typically lasts three hours and constitutes a 'guided self-exploration' for the client, prompted by questions and reflections from the coach. Its most important task is to build a working alliance between the client and coach. For that reason, the coach may be well advised to work with the client's 'story' as it naturally unfolds. Although we suggest to clients that they start with describing the beginning of their lives and work forward chronologically (partly for clarity and partly because this is the order in which the influences upon the client accumulated throughout his or her life), and use a template to prompt ourselves (see Box 5.1), we usually find that we move away from this at some point during the review.

As we guide our clients through this process, we are aware that we are jumping in at the deep end of this new relationship. Some clients find the prospect of talking about themselves for three hours daunting, while others enjoy it. We try to stay attuned and in communication with our clients and their experience of this review process as an important first step in the entire coaching process. It is important that the client feels respected, understood and supported, so we seek to ensure that our clients maintain control of the process and ownership of any arising insights or issues.

Box 5.1

As the client relates his or her life story we aim to cover three areas flexing around the client's account of his or her life:

1. **Exploration of self**
   - Family background
   - Educational and career histories
   - Current personal life
   - Values, attitudes and beliefs

2. **Exploration of context**
   - Organisational overview (including values, culture, vision, strategy)
   - The Board or management team's role and purpose ('content')
   - The Board or management team's relationships, dynamics and effectiveness, and their role within this ('process')

3. **Exploration of role and performance**
   - His or her role and key objectives
   - His or her key stakeholders
   - How he or she is evaluated, and by whom
   - Skills self-assessment
   - His or her own team and his or her assessment of its functioning

During the review, some coaches draw upon particular diagnostics or data gathering methods, such as:

- psychometric tests (for example Myers-Briggs, Firo-B)

- 360-degree feedback (of widely varying depth, sometimes including face-to-face interviews by the coach of key colleagues and even external stakeholders and family members)

- shadowing of the executive to observe his or her behaviour in the workplace

While this can be a very informative process, we believe that extensive initial data gathering should be approached with caution as it involves some potential risks:

- It can place the locus of evaluation externally and not enough within the executive

- It can prove overwhelming to the client receiving such abundant (and usually unprecedented) feedback

- It can be a process driven by the coach

- It can get in the way of the coach and client developing a relationship and their own feedback system

- It can delay faster development by getting caught up in 'analysis paralysis'

To mitigate these risks, the coach, sponsor and client should agree from the start how much assessment would be useful.

During the review, any development needs are noted by the client and coach. Towards the end of the meeting, these are shaped into the coaching contract, with clear objectives and measures of success defined against them.

Sharing of the 'Triangular Contract'

After the meeting, the coach usually takes responsibility for drafting the coaching contract on the basis of the review meeting and sends it to the client for approval. When the client has approved the contract, the coach then writes to the sponsor (copying the client), confirming:

- when the coach first met the client (that is, date of exploratory meeting) and when the review session took place

- that the client wishes to undertake a coaching programme

- the coaching contract (that is, objectives and measures for success)

- the exact terms of the programme, including the anticipated duration (for example a year), whether the coach is undertaking to provide unlimited or specific hours of contact over that time, how often the coach recommends to the client that they meet

- the coaching fee and terms of payment

- when the sponsor can next expect to hear from the coach (to review progress)

The Work

In the last chapter, we illustrated the nature of the work once the coaching has begun. There are two elements that we would like to make more explicit here:

- *Session management* (managing the 'micro process')
- *'Behind-the-scenes support'* (what the coach should have in place to ensure rigour and professional support)

Session Management

Although the coach will meet his or her client at the start of each session open to whatever the client might wish to address, the coach will wish to maintain a minimum structure to manage each session effectively. After a client's usual brief update (that is, anything significant that has transpired since the last meeting), the coach may seek to follow up on any action agreed at the last session and identify objectives for this session. These may refer to the coaching contract or include something that has emerged since which the client regards as more important or topical to address.

As the session (typically an hour or an hour and a half) is drawing to a close, the coach will wish to alert the client to the fact that the session is near its end, and will leave a few minutes at the end when he or she asks the client to summarise what the client will be taking away from the session (as learning or action).

The session management process is likely to be similar, whether the coach and client are working face-to-face or over the telephone.

'Behind-the-Scenes' Support

There are certain ways that assist the coach in supporting his or her ongoing practice with clients:

- *Session notes and preparation:* after all sessions with clients, the coach will wish to make his or her own notes about the session, which act as a combination of an aide memoire and a vehicle for reflecting upon the coaching process and relationship. Such notes might involve a combination of 'content' and 'process' observations, and cover some or all of the following:

- The facts about the client's current situation/context
- The session's objectives
- How those objectives were addressed (that is, 'how we worked together today')
- Any significant learning (on either part)
- Any action agreed
- Any provisional task for next session
- The coach's reflections on the process and relationship (for example what seems to be going well and not so well, what issues to take to supervision)

Such notes also enable the coach to prepare for the next session, to get back into the client's context at the start of the next session, and, if appropriate, think about any topic the client wished to address in advance of the session.

■ *Supervision:* by its very nature, development coaching operates behind closed doors with little opportunity for direct scrutiny or outside feedback. Professional coaches have therefore borrowed a model from psychotherapy in which psychotherapists and counsellors contract with a third party expert (usually a more experienced practitioner) to review their work with clients. In a therapeutic setting, the guidelines are one hour of supervision to every six hours of client contact. For coaches under training, this may represent a sensible frequency. For experienced coaches, the amount of time devoted to supervision is perhaps best arrived at in discussion with a potential supervisor in the light of the size and complexity of the client case load. There will be further discussion of supervision in Chapter 8.

Ongoing Review and Evaluation

Normally, halfway through the contract (in terms of either time elapsed or number of hours spent together), a formal progress review with the client is desirable. Box 5.2 indicates the kind of structure and questions which may be used to elicit feedback.

By the end of the halfway review session, the coach should undertake to re-contract for the remainder of the work with the client. The coach should also recommend that the client shares his or her feedback and new contract with the organisational sponsor (if there is one), or may suggest meeting with the sponsor together to provide a progress report.

Box 5.2

Client's feedback

I would find it very useful to hear your feedback, for example:

- How is our relationship going, from your perspective?
- What were your first impressions (for example on reflection, how helpful was my description of how I work during our first meeting)?
- How did you find the review process? How relevant have you found it?
- What has been helpful?
- What has been unhelpful?
- What would have been helpful?
- How have you experienced me?

Coach's feedback

Would you like to hear my feedback about you and our work together?

- My first impressions of you were …
- My sense of our early work was …
- My experience was that this changed in that …
- My perceptions of milestones in our process/relationship were …

Programme review

- Reflecting back on our original agenda, how are we doing against your objectives?
- If we haven't addressed as many of the objectives as we expected (to have at this stage), is this for good reason (for example changing circumstances/priorities)?
- What do you feel you have learned?
- Have any particular milestones or 'aha moments' stood out during the process?

Where do we go from here?

- We have (xx more time) left; what would you still like to achieve?

Finally, the coach may wish to take the feedback from the halfway review process to supervision in order to explore areas for improving his or her practice, with this client and others.

Ending and Managing Feedback to the Organisation

The end of a development coaching contract is a significant event. If the work has been meaningful and effective, both coach and client are likely to regard their relationship as a significant one and therefore to have strong feelings about its ending. In many ways, the ending is a microcosm of the overall process. The more profound the learning process and relationship between coach and client has been, the more important the ending is likely to be.

There is both a business and a personal dimension to the ending process. At least two coaching sessions may be needed to provide enough time, space and attention to this significant event. There are four important elements to manage regarding ending:

1. Evaluating the process and outcomes (the 'business' dimension)
2. Achieving a proper closure to the relationship (the 'personal' dimension)
3. Providing feedback to the organisational sponsor
4. Identifying future contact, where appropriate

Evaluating the Process and Outcomes

The business element of the ending tends to follow a similar format to the halfway review process. Both client and coach should review their objectives (original and revised) and discuss what has been achieved together and what the client may need to continue working on in the future, and the extent to which the work has been satisfactory from the point of view of both the individual and his or her organisation.

Achieving a Proper Closure to the Relationship

The personal element of the ending is more complex. Much writing in the psychotherapy world has been devoted to the subject of endings and the deep-rooted feelings that accompany them. While a coaching relationship may not necessarily entail the depth of feeling involved in a psychotherapeutic relationship, it is important for a coach not to underestimate the significance of the relationship and therefore the time it may take for some clients to realise what the ending is about.

The client may deny that significance, for to acknowledge it is to acknowledge a loss. In this case, the client runs the risk of not absorbing important aspects of the learning after the coaching relationship has ended. The coach may be well advised, therefore, to dwell on the changes that have taken place and the fact that these have come about reciprocally, from the mutual contribution of both to the relationship and to the learning. Indeed, the client may not see what he or she has contributed unless this is pointed out by the coach, so that the client can acknowledge it and own it for him or herself. For the same reason, the coach needs to name how he or she feels about the ending in order to allow the client to do the same. A client may then be able to celebrate what has been learned and to distinguish between the contributions of the client and the coach to that learning.

As the purpose of development coaching is to enhance the client's functioning and autonomy, the aim of the coach will be to make him or herself redundant to the client. Any future coaching relationship needs some justification, therefore, and may more successfully be entered into if there is a gap between the end of the first contract and the start of the second, followed by a meeting to review the consolidation of the client's learning before agreeing the new objectives.

Providing Feedback to the Organisation

The organisation paying for the contract must receive, and perceive, a sufficient return on investment. Thus, it is important that at the end of a contract, feedback and evaluation are provided to the organisational sponsor, as well (when he or she is not the client).

As with the halfway review, the coach will encourage the client to provide feedback to the sponsor. But the coach may also wish to communicate with the sponsor directly, to find out how he or she has perceived the process and its value. In feedback to sponsors, the coach will attempt to ensure that he or she says (or writes) nothing that has not been shared first with the client.

Identifying Appropriate Future Contact

Once sufficient attention has been given to ending the original contract, it may be appropriate to discuss future opportunities for continuing to work with a client. There are two possible indications for this:

■ *New development needs:* it may be appropriate to consider a new contract in the future, provided the client has consolidated his or her learning from the original coaching and if client, coach and sponsor are able to identify new development needs that might best be addressed by development coaching. In addition, a change in a client's personal circumstances (for example a promotion) may indicate an appropriate reason for returning to coaching.

■ *The benefit of ongoing 'sounding board' support:* in some cases, particularly with a CEO or other senior individual isolated by his or her position from feedback or the ability to test thinking, the client may value a 'retainer' contract. This is a contract to meet as necessary to act as a sounding board and test/challenge the client's thinking. Where the existing coaching relationship works well, and the coach has acquired a high level of organisational understanding, such an arrangement may be seen as beneficial.

Summary

This chapter has considered the processes involved in a typical professional development coaching contract. It has outlined the stages in relationship management with the sponsoring organisation: exploration, contracting, review and ending – and has described the tasks of each of these stages. It has detailed the processes involved in working with the client over the life of the contract, and of reviewing that work together. Finally, it has highlighted the importance of the ending in coaching and the task of this stage.

In Chapter 6, we consider the competencies required of the professional development coach and how and where these are best acquired.

The Required Competencies

We have looked at the theory behind development coaching with a particular focus on leadership. We have examined three case studies illustrating the work and have outlined the processes involved in a typical coaching contract. In order to provide the basis against which the reader may assess a potential coach and/or his or her own fit with this growing profession, we now review the competencies required of a professional development coach: the knowledge, understanding and skills involved.

Drawing upon the Marriage of Consulting and Counselling

In Chapter 3, we described development coaching as a marriage of two disciplines: consulting and counselling, which can be viewed as a continuum. The coach works continually along this continuum, as illustrated in Figure 6.1.

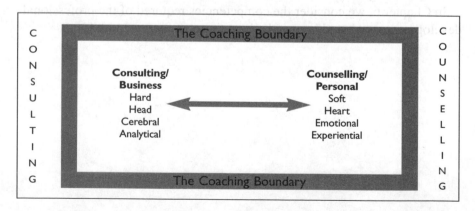

Figure 6.1 A consulting to counselling continuum of coaching

Table 6.1 The consulting and counselling competencies relevant to coaching

	Consulting	Counselling
Knowledge of:	■ current business developments and issues ■ business processes and systems ■ management theory and practice ■ behavioural sciences (especially re consultancy process and change)	■ human growth and development ■ the process of individual learning and transformation ■ the range of counselling or therapeutic approaches
Understanding of:	■ the business environment ■ organisational dynamics ■ the human and behavioural aspects of the consulting process and the consultant–client relationship	■ the process of individual change ■ at least one counselling or therapeutic method in some depth

Skills in:	*Content*
	■ framing and making sense of complexity
	■ analysis and problem solving
	■ creative thinking
	
	Process
	■ maintaining a mode of 'experimental flexibility'
	■ communicating, building trust and negotiating
	■ generating and facilitating change in people and in organisations
		■ maintaining personal congruence (realness) within the professional relationship
		■ maintaining an ability to accept unconditionally the client as a person
		■ maintaining an ability to empathise with and understand the other's world
		■ active listening, for example
		  ■ clarifying and reflecting
		  ■ open and non-judgemental questioning
		  ■ summarising to check understanding
		  ■ appropriately challenging the other's thinking and assumptions

The coach draws on particular knowledge (information and theoretical frameworks), understanding (the synthesis of knowledge and experience) and skills from both these disciplines. These are summarised in Table 6.1.

We distinguish here between content (hard) and process (soft) skills in consulting. At the soft (process) end, there is much convergence with the counselling skills shown. A description of the training for process consulting skills by Arthur Turner implies the overlaps between coaching, consulting and counselling:

The three most relevant skills to develop for an effective consulting process are, in my opinion: diagnosing behaviour, listening, and behaving authentically.

Diagnostic skill is developed by examining and discussing what is taking place within client organisations. These discussions develop hypotheses that can be tested in subsequent client contacts. In such discussions and experiments with different approaches, consultants may discover, perhaps to their discomfort, that effective diagnosis of behaviour is often in part an intuitive and not just a logical process.

Listening of a very special kind is an essential consulting process skill. Good consultants learn how to listen with understanding to what is meant as well as to what is said, to feelings as well as to facts, to what is hard to admit and not just easy to say ...

Behaving authentically needs to be seen as an equally necessary skill. Consultants need to be able to be themselves, to behave according to their own values, and sometimes confront clients with unwelcome facts and opinions.[1]

Thus, the disciplines of consulting and counselling contribute substantially to the activity of coaching, and, particularly in the area of process skills, overlap significantly. However, what is unique or characteristic of coaching is the way in which these skills are applied so as to facilitate the client's learning.

Facilitating the Client's Learning

Fundamental Conditions for Development Coaching

In order to facilitate the client's learning, we suggest that provision of the following conditions (which draw upon the above skills) is fundamental to development coaching:

- psychological space
- support
- challenge

Psychological Space

In order to be able to reflect, to make connections between thinking and feeling, and to make new sense of one's working situation, space for such perspective is needed. That space is essentially psychological (although physical separation from the work context does help the process). It is provided by the coach bringing him or herself authentically to the coaching encounter, not seeking to direct the client and using active listening skills responsively (especially that of reflecting). To be able to create this space for the client requires of the coach that he or she be not in awe of the client nor seeking to gain the client's approval or admiration. The task is to be genuinely neutral – to be an undistorting reflecting glass. And this means accepting the client as an individual without judgement. To achieve this implies a high level of *self*-acceptance on the part of the coach, and humility – recognition that it is the client who does the work and achieves the results.

Support

Coaching, as we have said, is essentially a collaborative activity, in which clients are free to reflect on themselves and their context without needing to defend themselves from judgement, because the coach is able to offer the conditions for such openness. Those conditions include offering the client the experience of being 'heard' – through empathy, which the coach is able to communicate, and through being valued or prized by the coach. This is not an attitude that the coach can 'put on'. It arises out of real understanding of the client and his or her working context, and most importantly, out of the coach's openness to his or her own emotions and emotional responses to the client. The coaching relationship is one of real, although boundaried, intimacy.

Challenge

A main aim of coaching is to enable the client to challenge his or her existing mental frameworks and forms of thought, in order to encourage the making of new connections in thinking, and between thinking and feeling. An important skill for the coach is to offer challenge effectively and appropriately. This involves the ability to frame issues, focus thought through incisive questioning and feed back honestly but respectfully reactions to the 'theories' clients form regarding their 'world' and the action they intend. To do this effectively requires good understanding of the work and industry context on the part of the coach, as well as insight into his or her client, him or herself, and into the dynamic between client and coach in the moment and over time.

In facilitating the client's learning in development coaching, these conditions may be translated into the skills and underlying requirements outlined in Table 6.2.

Table 6.2 Coaching specific skills and underlying requirements		
Condition	**Coach Skill/State**	**Underlying Requirement**
Psychological Space	Authenticity/congruence	Profound self-awareness
	Non-directiveness	Self-acceptance
	Active listening and reflecting	No awe of the client or desire for power by association
		Understanding and bracketing of one's own thoughts and feelings (non-judgementalism)
		Humility
Support	Unconditional positive regard for the client	Understanding (and experience) of the context of, and demands on, the client
	Empathy	Being open to one's own and the other's (emotional) experiencing
		Prizing of the other
		Warmth towards the other
Challenge	Focused questioning	Industry insight
	Honest feedback	Psychological insight (into oneself, the client, the relationship between the coach and the client)
	Framing issues	Respect for the client

The coaching skills outlined under *psychological space* and *support* draw more from the counselling end of the continuum. Under *challenge*, the consultancy end comes more into play. But both are blended. The underlying requirements imply considerable personal maturity and self-awareness in the coach. The fact that the coach may have had experience in the role or situation of the client, while not critical, may help in achieving closer, quicker and more accurate ability to empathise or 'tune in'. It may also assist in focusing the work of the session more sharply.

Specific Coaching Skills

While coaching draws most of its skills, and all of its knowledge and understanding, from other disciplines, there is a range of skills which are specific to coaching itself. These are:

- skills in the overall management of the coaching programme or contract (the 'macro process')
- skills in the management of each individual coaching session (the 'micro process')

Skills in Programme and Contract Management

Managing the Sponsor's Expectations

The development coach should be competent to:

- Document the initial briefing about the client
- Keep the sponsoring organisation informed of progress/issues arising
- Facilitate the client's direct feedback to their sponsoring organisation
- Feed back to the sponsor (within the bounds of confidentiality agreed)
- Set in place the monitoring framework and use this to analyse/demonstrate added value to the organisation at the end of the contract

Managing Client's Expectations

The development coach should be competent to:

- Provide a clear description of coaching in the exploratory meeting
- Document the client's initial expectation of the process and create a contract with clear programme objectives and measurable targets
- Manage the balance between individual and corporate interest with the client
- Facilitate closure at the end of the contract

Let us briefly illustrate the sponsor and client relationship management skills required in the contracting process (mentioned in Chapter 5) from work with one of our clients. Initially, the coach spent time with the individual's chief executive (who had sponsored previous clients), helping him to articulate the development objectives for the individual from the chief executive's perspective (developing interpersonal managing skills with his reports and contributing more fully to group strategic thinking). The coach subsequently undertook an exploratory meeting with the prospective client to identify the client's objectives (as above, but developing the qualities and constituency for promotion to the Group Board), and then arranged for a meeting between coach, chief executive and client. In the three-way meeting, the client outlined his objectives for the proposed coaching for comment by the chief executive, and the chief executive elaborated his expectations in more detail. The coach's role was to introduce the meeting, facilitate the discussion between the individual and chief executive, summarise the contract as finally agreed and get commitment from the chief executive and the client to meet with the coach to review progress halfway through the contract and again at the end to discuss the success of the coaching contract/return on investment by the company. This process, while time consuming, had the effect of achieving great transparency in expectations and very high commitment to the process from both chief executive and client.

At the end of the contract, the client and coach were able to acknowledge the achievement of the client in letting go of a deeply rooted defensiveness with others and learning to listen with good openness, as well as the contribution that the challenge and substantial support of the coach made to facing the personal risk that this involved.

Managing the 'Macro Process'

In order that the process of the contract be managed well, the coach should be able to:

- Periodically measure progress against contract objectives

- Maintain appropriate frequency and duration of the sessions making up the contract

- Encourage and support clients seeking feedback from colleagues (for example 360-degree)

- Address any process/relationship issues that may occur (for example recurring absences/cancellations)

- Manage the balance between the original contract objectives and emerging issues or objectives

- Recognise when to refer to other services

In the case of Garry Parsons, described in Chapter 4, the objectives developed well beyond the original objectives of the contract, which had been essentially to assist him to manage his current responsibilities well and prepare for a future, more senior role. By the end of the coaching process, the focus of the work had become to develop him for the role of chief executive, something well outside his expectations nine months previously. This meant for the coach: helping Garry understand how his learning in the earlier part of the coaching applied to the top job, and helping him to maintain his sense of, and confidence in, himself and in his judgement in the face of sharply increased visibility to the Board and investor community.

Session Management

In order to manage the micro process of each session, the coach should be competent to:

- Agree objectives at the start of each session
- Manage the utilisation of time in each session to maximise the value to the client
- Facilitate summarisation at the end of each session
- Document content and process (including relationship) issues in client notes

In Chapter 5 we mentioned the place of summarisation in session management. We believe this is an especially important skill for the coach to develop. We use it at the outset of a session to capture the essence of the update that we encourage the client to offer. As the session develops, we use it both to capture the discussion or learning so far and to reflect our sense of the emotional responding we have noticed in the client during the discussion. We routinely use it at the end of each session, often after we have asked the client to comment on what they will take away from the session, both to anchor the learning and to give feedback on the experience we have had in the session.

Developing the Coaching Competencies

Competencies at the Consultancy End of the Continuum

These competencies are likely to be acquired in the coach's previous career or activity. Experience and/or understanding of business and organisational dynamics is most usually and conveniently acquired through the experience of working at a senior level in, most desirably, several organisational contexts. It is likely that this experience will have involved internal consultancy or project management from which skills in analysis, negotiation and planning will have been developed. A background in consultancy or senior operational or strategic management is particularly helpful.

Our own backgrounds are not untypical. One of us had early experience in the development and training of senior Prison Service staff (in association with Manchester Business School), followed by experience in management and consultancy at a senior level in government. He subsequently managed a retail chain and, in conjunction with this, developed a specialist consultancy. The other had an early career in public relations, followed by a full-time MBA at London Business School. She then worked as a consultant specialising in post-merger integration with Andersen Consulting (now Accenture).

Competencies at the Counselling End of the Continuum

While many coaches argue that it is not the coach's role to understand why clients do what they do, we believe that profound change of the kind which development coaching seeks to facilitate is difficult to achieve without a fairly sophisticated notion of human behaviour, from whatever orientation it may come. The question for people considering coaching as a career is, therefore, how they acquire a knowledge and understanding of human development and how they develop the self-awareness to become professionally competent to collaborate with their clients in the way we have just described.

In Chapter 9, Myles Downey has described three possible routes into coaching and, in Chapter 8, Beverly Brooks has laid stress on the importance of supervision as a means of furthering the learning and development of the coach. The most obvious way of acquiring these skills, which lie at the heart of coaching, is through training as a counsellor or therapist. Our own counselling training took place while practising as senior executive coaches. We have found that the insight and, more importantly, the process of expanding our self-awareness that that training offered us, have contributed substantially to the effectiveness of our work.

Counselling training, as a matter of course, provides the theory to underpin the understanding of human behaviour and of individual development. Most importantly, if it is a course that offers a substantial component of experiential learning (group work, role playing, a requirement to undergo personal therapy), it will provide a very useful context for developing skills at the counselling end of the continuum and the self-awareness involved. The humanistic frame of reference from which we basically operate (person-centred), offers a particularly good fit with the activity of coaching. For it works from a presumption that the individual has great potentiality and inherently seeks to give that potentiality expression and its primary focus is very much the healthy, creative core of the person.

We would recommend to anyone considering taking up coaching as a career who has not had this experience, to thoroughly research the therapeutic/counselling training available and seek to undertake it in parallel with training by the routes described in Chapters 8 and 9. In Appendix 2 we outline the basic approaches. The British Association for Counselling and Psychotherapy (BACP) publishes annually a comprehensive guide to the counselling and psychotherapy courses available throughout the United Kingdom.[2] It is probably wise to select a course that has been accredited by the BACP or a comparable body and, as stated, one with a strong component of experiential learning. Most courses will run an introductory seminar or selection day. Try more than one of these as the time and financial commitment in undertaking such training will be considerable (in our case, four years).

Competencies Specific to Professional Coaching for Leadership Development

In Chapter 3, we referred to the core activities involved in development coaching with a particular focus on developing leadership, as assisting the individual leader to develop greater 'bandwidth' and assisting him or her to develop authenticity – becoming open to the whole of his or her experiencing. We suggested that the coach focusing with the leader on his or her leadership task will pay particular attention to helping the leader to:

■ reflect on current experience

■ articulate his or her understanding of the organisation and test his or her internal response against the connections or insights so articulated

■ become open and sensitised to the play of his or her emotions and intuition in response to the events he or she is experiencing

■ 'thinker': move towards an experimental mode in which action and thought are held in parallel process

These are, of course, core development coaching competencies, not specific to coaching for leadership per se. When we talk about coaching for leadership, we are therefore talking about a particular *focus* of development coaching, rather than a specific *form* of coaching.

With all clients in leadership positions, the coach's aim is to assist them to make deeper sense of the world or organisation around them, to experiment or test their understanding in practice ('thinker') and to help them to develop a greater flexibility in responding. Essentially, the coach is trying to help the client 'shake the kaleidoscope' of his or her perception and mindset, and act on the new picture that emerges. Specifically, the coach seeks to notice connections between elements in the client's world and between his or her thinking and feeling and bring this into the client's awareness. And this may involve challenge to the client's current assumptions, as well as questioning what is happening in the 'here and now' between coach and client. This process is described well by Witherspoon when he talks of 'reflecting-in-action':

> Reflecting-in-action is a core competency for executive coaching. It refers to the paradoxical ability to step outside immediate events while still in them through a process of on the spot reflection and experimentation. The skill is instrumental for helping clients in the moment to produce valid information, informed choice and internal commitment.[3]

The other particular focus of coaching for leadership is assisting the client in becoming fully authentic. The expectations of the workplace and of upbringing often militate against this. To assist the client with this process, the coach, as we have indicated earlier, must be authentic – be him or herself. In the presence of a client, this can be a challenging process for it requires the parallel activities of attending to the client and what is going on within him or her and within his or her thinking, while concurrently attending in the same way to oneself. One gains competence of this kind purely by practice. Further, the coach needs to be prepared to trust in the client's process of becoming, which involves noticing the client as he or she becomes him or herself and prizing that. Being real in this way implies a considerable investment in personal development on the part of the coach.

The question remains as to whether there are any specific competencies a coach requires when working with very senior leaders. We think not. The chief executive of a large organisation may seek certain experience and background from his or her coach – who has to demonstrate credibility at this level. But, as we have said, this will be more about meeting the chief executive's preconditions for entertaining coaching than about any specific competence. However, as it is important for the coach to feel secure in his or her ability to work/add value with these often demanding clients occupying very exposed roles, then experience counts. By experience, we mean having occupied similar situations as the client and/or having worked with a wide range of clients and business situations, which will have increased the coach's ability to understand, and to be able to *demonstrate* an in-depth understanding of the client's business. Thus, extensive life and coaching experience and the wisdom that should develop with this are qualifications for working at the top level. In that sense, 'grey hairs' can be representative of something valuable.

Summary

In this chapter, we have reviewed the competencies (knowledge, understanding and skills) required to undertake professional development coaching. We have identified the competencies drawn from consulting and counselling, respectively, and those specific to development coaching: managing the 'macro' process of contract management, the 'micro' process of session management, and, most importantly, the competencies involved in facilitating the client's learning. We have looked briefly at the competencies required specifically in coaching for leadership.

Finally, we have reviewed where the competencies outlined may best be acquired. We have recommended that those thinking about professional development coaching as a career, and who have little knowledge of human growth, development and transition, research counselling/ psychotherapy training as a convenient and thorough source for acquiring such background and the personal development required.

Notes

1. Technical note in M. Kubr, *Management Consulting: A Guide to the Profession*, 2nd edn (Geneva: International Labour Office, 1986) p. 484.
2. *The Training in Counselling and Psychotherapy Directory* (Rugby: British Association for Counselling and Psychotherapy, 2001).
3. R. Witherspoon, 'Starting Smart: Clarifying Coaching Goals and Roles', in M. Goldsmith, L. Lyons and A. Freas (eds) *Coaching for Leadership: How the World's Greatest Coaches Help Leaders Learn* (San Francisco: Jossey-Bass, 2000) p. 178.

PART III

Key Issues within Professional Coaching for Leadership Development

In Part III, we have invited three very experienced practitioners to address three fundamental areas that the emerging profession of development coaching must address if it is to grow successfully – evaluation, ethics and training – and to explore the issues involved. Coaching is a 'soft' process and is therefore not easily susceptible to 'hard' measurement. However, if development coaching is to prosper, it will need to find ways to demonstrate the value it claims to add. Similarly, the credibility of the profession will depend on the rigour with which development coaching establishes an ethical framework and maintains it, and on the credentials of those offering this service.

CHAPTER 7

Evaluating Development Coaching

Glenn Whitney, ECD Insight

Noticing – much less measuring – change in human behaviour is a difficult undertaking. Yet professional coaching for leadership development is all about change – fostering it, celebrating it and highlighting it. Those who participate in development coaching and those who pay for it have a right to expect measurable changes.

In today's bottom-line driven business climate, any organisational consulting activities must be able to clearly demonstrate their efficacy and their cost effectiveness. Although development coaching is increasingly enjoying widespread acceptance, it will be progressively more challenged by its clients to *prove* its added value.

Yet many of the claims of the coaching profession to date revolve essentially around the statement – 'coaching is helpful because clients say it is helpful'. Left unanswered are key questions such as:

- How helpful?
- Helpful in what way?
- Who is/are the client(s)?
- Do key people the client relates with agree that coaching has been helpful?
- How cost effective is coaching?
- What alternatives to coaching exist to achieve similar (or better) results?

These questions are of vital importance to organisations deciding whether to invest tens of thousand of dollars in a process that is still somewhat shrouded in mystery.

In due course, professional coaching will need to demonstrate its efficacy in direct comparison to alternative forms of leadership development (for example MBAs, group-based development programmes). But, before it can do this, it first needs to address how to measure and evaluate its contribution in its own right.

This chapter therefore addresses the task for the coaching profession implied by this challenge by:

- Describing the different ways in which coaching may be evaluated and what evaluation has been conducted to date

- Describing how coaching and/or sponsoring organisations might most realistically begin to address the need for more rigorous evaluation

There appears to be a continuum along which the evaluation of coaching can take place, ranging from a 'micro' to 'macro' scope, as illustrated in Figure 7.1.

Individual Contracting

At the most 'micro' level, coaching can be evaluated on a programme-by-programme basis. As has been described in Chapter 5, the platform for the coaching process is the 'triangular contract' between the sponsoring organisation, the coach and the client, against which everyone may evaluate progress. The more precise the goals of a coaching programme, as defined in the coaching contract, the more possible it will be to measure the results.

Although clear contracting represents the best method for evaluating an individual development coaching programme, it is worth mentioning that

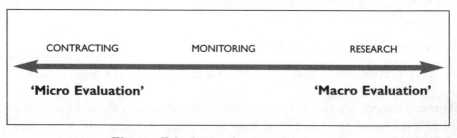

Figure 7.1 An 'evaluation continuum'

there are several challenges inherent in this 'micro evaluation' of development coaching, even when based upon best practice contracting. These include:

- Achieving agreement with all stakeholders about who is/are the client(s), including balancing the interests of the individual and the organisation (for example who should ultimately measure success – the client, the coach, the organisation or a mixture of all three?)

- Achieving sufficient clarity of the coaching goals, given that the development areas which coaching addresses are often inherently ambiguous (for example how do you measure goals such as 'to improve my relationships with my key stakeholders'?)

- Accommodating the inherently – and appropriately – shifting and emerging nature of development coaching contracts and goals

- Adapting to the inevitable changes in the individual's environment and contexts over the period of a year (for example the impact of a merger or a promotion upon the client and his or her development goals)

- Allowing for the variations in coaches' styles and methods (for example even if one coach's work with a client has been deemed as beneficial, it does not mean that another coach will have equal 'success' with the next client referred by the organisation)

- Allowing for the individuality of each coaching relationship (for example just because one coach worked effectively with a client does not mean that he or she will work well with the next client)

In addition, there are a couple of additional limitations inherent in the evaluation of each development programme. First, there is usually a very small 'universe' of assessors (typically the client, coach and organisational sponsor), which inevitably magnifies the opinions of each one and therefore potentially distorts the picture.

Second, there is an inescapable subjectivity or bias within those assessors. It is a well-known phenomenon in psychotherapy and counselling research that most clients will judge the process as worthwhile and effective to some degree. This is something of a truism – if they did not think counselling effective, they would not stay in counselling in the first place. The same is likely to be true of coaching. Although most coaches can display an impressive collection of testimonials from current or previous clients attesting to the utility of the process, again, we know there is a pervasive bias to judge as valuable any experience we have gone through, particularly if it has been strenuous and/or financially expensive. Coaches who survey their clients immediately after a programme as to the utility of that intervention are particularly powerfully subject to this bias.

These challenges and limitations mean that even the micro evaluation of individual development coaching programmes, with a narrow scope, is destined to be an inexact science at best.

Outcome Research

At the other end of the continuum is the most 'macro' form of evaluation or what might be termed outcome research.

To date, there appears to have been virtually no formal research into the effects of any type of coaching, let alone development coaching. One study by David Peterson at Personnel Decisions International (PDI) studied 370 participants in their coaching programmes over a five-year period.[1] Both participants and their managers reported significant improvement in new skills, and more importantly, in overall performance on the job. Peterson compared the results of his study with a study of other management development methods by Burke and Day.[2] Using 'effect size' (a measure of the amount of change that occurred), Peterson concluded that the coaching produced approximately three times as much change as the management development methods studied by Burke and Day. It is, however, important to be careful in drawing extensive conclusions from a single study, and these findings have yet to be replicated in any published studies.

Since there is such a dearth of research into coaching, it seems appropriate to look to some of the disciplines most closely related to development coaching to see if any lessons can be learned from these. There seem two obvious areas to look:

1.   Psychotherapy and counselling

2.   Management development and training

Psychotherapy and Counselling

Although it is perhaps surprising that the coaching profession has attempted so little study or formal evaluation of its activities, development coaching does operate in the world of the human psyche, adopting the practices and research traditions of the social sciences, particularly psychotherapy and counselling.

Nearly a century of psychotherapy and counselling research has consistently demonstrated its effectiveness as a process that can diminish anxiety, depression, phobias and many other forms of psychic distress. Indeed, even faced with the competition of powerful biochemical psychiatric medication, psychotherapy has proven itself to be as effective, and at times more effective, than anything the pharmaceutical companies can manufacture.

However, psychotherapy and counselling have consistently failed to demonstrate definitively and objectively why they are effective, when they are effective, for whom they are effective and what precisely their effective practice should be. There are literally hundreds of major competing 'brands' of psychotherapy, all claiming excellent, demonstrable results. Most suggest their brand of psychotherapy is more effective than the others. And yet, as researchers like Lambert have pointed out, no broadly accepted series of studies has yet demonstrated the superior efficacy of one particular method.[3]

Even the elegantly written, groundbreaking case studies Sigmund Freud presented to demonstrate the effectiveness of the psychoanalytic method have since been called into serious question. Researchers and writers such as Masson,[4] F. Crews[5] and Stadlen[6] have debunked many of the grandiose claims Freud made for his 'talking cure'. It turns out that, seen through somewhat more objective lenses than those of the great therapist himself, many of the famous cases made few, if any, sustainable improvements. By interviewing patients and their family members years after treatment, the researchers have cast doubts on Freud's claims of having effected significant behaviour changes. There are important lessons to be learned here for the practice of coaching. In effect, what this form of outcome research has shown is that, judged from the outside, changes that the client's *coach* sees as significant may be absent or of scant significance.

Management Development and Training

There has also been a handful of studies in the wider field of management development and training that suggest that activities akin to coaching are effective – that is they accomplish their intended goal. For example, Morrow has demonstrated the economic utility of corporate-wide training.[7] Dixon and Young positively evaluated a programme to help leaders take effective action at the Center for Creative Leadership in Greensboro, North Carolina.[8]

Increasingly, however, academic critics are bemoaning the dearth of research in the area of behaviour change, including Fiedler[9] who has asserted that many leading management development programmes are untested and of uncertain value. In Goleman's exhaustive review of programmes that develop 'emotional intelligence' in the workplace,[10] he has suggested that many of these training activities are of dubious value. Estimates of the extent to which skills taught in company training programmes carry over into day-to-day practice on the job are as low as 10%. Goleman calls much of corporate training and development a 'billion-dollar mistake'.

One study cited by Goleman, of a five-day residential programme to improve the 'people skills' of the senior managers of a pharmaceuticals company found the managers were *worse* off than before the seminar.[11] When rated by their bosses afterwards, on average, the participants were judged to be 'a little less capable' than before the training. This study might be exceptional, but it underlines the fact that positive outcomes of executive development cannot be taken for granted. There is a clear need for all organisations to measure and evaluate the results of their coaching programme to ensure they deliver the intended results and to continually improve their effectiveness.

The most common source of evaluation data is participant evaluation sheets, as well as continued demand for that particular development method. This information is more akin to popularity polls than hard indicators of performance change, as Goleman notes. A survey of training in Fortune 500 companies by William Clegg in 1987, for instance, showed no correlation between participants' reports of satisfaction with management training and their learning or demonstrated improvement on the job – as one review put it: 'liking does not imply learning'.

Perhaps the closest example relevant to coaching of a study of management development is one (in press) by Ashridge Management School's Centre for Leadership Excellence. The centre runs a one-week residential management development programme that includes sessions with professional coaches during the week, as well as in follow-up sessions several months later. As such, it is not a standard, coaching-only programme and we should be somewhat cautious about making general statements about coaching from it. Nevertheless, the study has been diligently executed and is to be commended in that it surveyed participants six to 18 months after completion. This is considerably beyond the period when the potentially distorting positive 'after-glow' effect is particularly strong.

The Ashridge programme has many points in common with leadership development programmes at leading management schools around the world and therefore deserves to be looked at closely. The survey included the responses of 310 programme participants. Asked if their leadership had 'improved on a scale of 1 (no more effective) to 10 (very much more effective)', some 90% responded 5 or above, with 55% reporting 7 or above. Some 55% of the participants felt the programme made them 'very much more effective' leaders. For 79% the programme provided 'much greater personal gain than they expected' and 74% found the coaching element to be 'extremely helpful'.

Turning specifically to the coaching component of the Ashridge programme, 96% of the participants rated meeting with their coach as 5 or above on a scale of 1 (not helpful) to 10 (extremely helpful). Some 70% rated the coaches 7 or above.

However, it is worth noting that these findings, although impressive, are consistent with the psychotherapy and counselling research mentioned earlier that consistently shows positive evaluations of clients towards their therapists. Personal evaluations are usually positive regardless of whether the clients are satisfied with the overall *outcome* of the counselling/therapy process.

It is also important to highlight that those surveyed for satisfaction levels in this study are primarily the participants. The only other stake-holders in the process surveyed are the coaches themselves. While this is unfortunate, it is not unusual. This reminds us of the ever-present issue of just who are the clients of corporate-sponsored coaching. While opinions from the participants about the utility of the Ashridge programme are certainly important, arguably as important are the opinions of the spon-sors, that is, the organisations footing the bill. Interestingly, the only refer-ence to sponsors in a preliminary report of the Ashridge study was that they were 'generally happy and the only consistent criticism was cost'.

Although there is clearly a need to conduct more research into coaching, it is sobering to observe that research efforts in more established disci-plines such as the two mentioned above have yielded very few definitive results to support the efficacy of their methods.

Indeed, the potential study in a rigorous manner of the outcomes of development coaching, ideally both within and across organisations, is fraught with potential problems. Any such study would suffer from a cumulative magnification of the same challenges mentioned earlier in this chapter under 'Individual Contracting' (for example variability, subjec-tivity/bias).

From a scientific standpoint, the ambiguity and complexity of the 'variables' to be measured arguably defy measurement. It is questionable whether even the best designed study could ever achieve 'like-for-like comparisons'. In addition, any study would have to include at least the following elements in its protocol:

- a sufficiently significant sample of coaching programmes/clients

- a sufficiently wide assessment population (that is, additional stake-holders around each client studied whose opinions might be solicited to reduce the subjectivity of a narrow sample of direct participants as described earlier)

- a control group against which to compare the 'coached sample'

A study of this scope and complexity would require a very substantial investment in time, effort and skills, and therefore only a limited number of organisations would have the resources and sufficient motivation to undertake such a study.

It is worth noting that, if an organisation or group of organisations were to undertake this kind of research, they might be well advised to begin with studying a series of performance rather than development coaching programmes (as defined in Chapter 1), as the coaching contracts and outcomes to be measured would at least be slightly more predictable and measurable.

Monitoring

So what might represent a more realistic alternative to a full-scale research study of development coaching? In the middle of the 'evaluation continuum' between contracting and research is what might be termed 'monitoring'. While not on as grand a scale as a research study, monitoring is intended to provide a better overview than the analysis of just one or two coaching programmes in isolation. Although monitoring is unlikely to provide as powerful an analysis of coaching's efficacy as a research study, it could provide the material for a less subjective assessment of the impact of coaching within an organisation, and, of course, could demonstrate to a current or potential sponsoring organisation that the coaching provider is committed to monitoring and evaluating the overall return on the sponsor's investment.

Such a monitoring programme could be designed to include the evaluation of five to ten coaching programmes provided to one sponsoring organisation by a coaching provider. This limited scope would enable a more realistic cross-comparison than a more complex and formal research study involving several sponsoring and coaching organisations.

Even though less complex than a formal outcome research study, a monitoring programme still raises several complex issues in its design, including:

■ How many, if any, diagnostics should be involved to assist the measurement of outcomes (for example before and after 360-degree feedback, psychometrics)?

■ How will such data be collected (for example questionnaires, interviews)?

■ How many stakeholders (beyond the 'triangular contract' of the client, coach and sponsor) should be involved?

■ Are the clients comfortable with the degree of scrutiny that the monitoring may involve for them, personally (that is, perhaps requiring more transparency of the coaching process than involved in the usual confidentiality agreement between coach and client)?

So what might a sample monitoring process look like? It might use as its benchmark a before and after 360-degree feedback process.[12] When the number of those surveyed is substantial, for instance 10 or 15, we can be more confident that we are getting a reasonably accurate overall picture.

Such a 360-degree feedback survey might be designed to measure the 'base-line' skills which each client and coach have identified for development as part of their contract. Depending on cost considerations, the survey can be conducted via questionnaires (either anonymously or not, depending on participant preferences) or interviewing (usually by the coach rather than the client to ensure sufficient candour). As long as the survey quantifies the responses in some way, it is then possible to compare 'scores' taken before a coaching programme and afterwards (and, ideally, six months after the programme's completion).

To be sure, the process is not flawless; it is subject to the goodwill and diligence of those giving the feedback. Nevertheless, the process is considerably more reliable than asking only clients to rate the utility of the coaching they have undergone or the extent to which they believe they have made positive changes.

Such surveys can be used for occasional monitoring by coaching or sponsoring organisations for quality control purposes when costs are an issue, or built into each coaching programme for programmes with less limited financial resources.

Conclusions

At the moment, coaching is enjoying increasing acceptance. But if this acceptance is to endure and deepen, the coaching profession will need to clearly demonstrate its added value. There is therefore an urgent need for practitioners and the organisational sponsors of coaching to more rigorously evaluate its outcomes.

To date, there have been very few published studies of any type of coaching. Although research is needed to justify the cost of coaching and to reassure reluctant clients of its utility, this chapter has identified the considerable challenges of such an undertaking. Perhaps more realistically, a well designed monitoring process in which more of the stakeholders in an executive's development are surveyed might be used to understand more about why, when and for whom coaching works and how to increase its effectiveness further.

Notes

1. D.B. Peterson, 'Skill learning and behavior change in an individually tailored management coaching and training program'. Unpublished doctoral dissertation (University of Minnesota, 1993).
2. M.J. Burke and R.R. Day, 'A Cumulative Study of the Effectiveness of Managerial Training', *Journal of Applied Psychology*, 1986, **71**: 232–46.
3. M.J. Lambert 'Implications of Outcome Research for Psychotherapy Integration', in J.C. Norcross and M.R. Goldfried (eds), *Handbook of Therapy Integration* (New York: Basic Books, 1992).
4. J. Masson, 'The Tyranny of Psycotherapy', in W. Dryden and C. Feltham (eds), *Psychotherapy and Its Discontents* (Buckingham: Open University Press, 1992).
5. F. Crews, *Memory Wars: Freud's Legacy in Dispute* (New York: New York Review of Books, 1997).
6. A. Stadlen 'Was Dora Ill?' in L. Spurling (ed.) *Sigmund Freud: Critical Assessments*, Vol. 2 (London: Routledge, 1989) pp. 196–203.
7. C. Morrow 'The Enlightened CEO's Demand: An Investigation on the Effect and Economic Utility of Corporate-Wide Training', *Personnel Psychology*, 1997, p. 50.
8. N.M. Dixon and D. Young, 'Helping Leaders Take Effective Action: Program Evaluation' (The Center for Creative Leadership, 1997).
9. F. Fiedler, 'Research on Leadership Selection and Training: One View of the Future', *Administrative Science Quarterly*, 1996, **11**: 239–58.
10. D. Goleman, *Working with Emotional Intelligence* (London: Bloomsbury, 1998).
11. N.M. Dixon and D. Young (1997) op.cit.
12. B. Underhill and M. Goldsmith, 'The Impact of Direct Report Feedback and Follow-up on Leadership Effectiveness', in D. Bracken, C. Timmreck and A. Church (eds) *The Handbook of Multisource Feedback: Comprehensive Resource for Designing and Implementing MsF Processes* (San Francisco: Jossey-Bass, 2001).

CHAPTER 8

Ethics and Standards in Coaching

Beverly Brooks, Penna Executive Coaching

A coach is a strange animal. Neither a trainer, whose contract is to impart knowledge and skills, nor a counsellor, whose main domain is the personal and interpersonal. The coach who is engaged in developmental work has strayed into a 'new' domain. Indeed, it could be argued that the activity is a new 'profession' and, as such, needs to look to how it conducts itself – the ethical considerations which guide its behaviour and the standards which it should seek to apply to the activity itself.

In considering these issues, I wish to offer no rules but to point up some of the difficulties that may lie in wait for the unsuspecting potential purchaser, or potential coach navigating a coaching relationship, and to assist them to arm themselves with some questions. The areas I will address relate to:

- who is the customer – the client or sponsoring company?

- the confidentiality of the coaching relationship

- the accountability of the coach when dealing with issues outside his or her competence

- the skills necessary for professional coaching and the ongoing development needs of the coach

- the supervision of the coach

It is not an exhaustive list, but may serve to indicate the coaching provider's level of thinking around such areas.

A Case Study

Let me illustrate some of the ethical dilemmas a coach may face with a case study. Fred is recognised within a company for his outstanding expertise within the finance area by promotion to the Board as director of finance. His CEO, with whom Fred plays golf, is anxious that Fred gets the best shot at this new promotion by offering him coaching. In an initial three-way meeting, the objectives set by the CEO are:

- helping Fred into his new role

- looking at how he impacts the Board and manages his relationships with other board members, the chairman and the non-executives

- helping him to maximise his team's efforts

Because the world is not perfect, Fred has been in the role for six months before this request is made and the CEO has spotted that there are what he calls 'teething problems', specifically clashes between Fred and the director of sales and marketing and the director of IT. Further, Fred has alienated his chief accountant who has resigned amid accusations of a 'picky, hands on' style, which constantly finds fault with the efforts of his team. The CEO only mentions these other areas in a phone call to the coach as he does not want to weaken Fred's confidence further by naming the issues in the three-way meeting and, anyway, 'he's a friend'.

At the assessment stage of the coaching programme, Fred confesses to finding things 'beyond' him. He feels that, although he is good at his job, there is a huge difference between being a 'good accountant' and being a 'good finance director' – notably the ability to think strategically and independently of the wishes of the CEO. Further, he does not feel he has the necessary 'soft skills' to manage the personalities involved – his team, the Board and so on, and feels less confident performing at this level than he does with the 'City types' he has to work with on occasion. He has responded by burying himself in detail, with a tendency to stick with what he knows (hence the 'picky, hands on' style loathed by his chief accountant) and protects himself at board level by becoming aggressive and argumentative when he feels his weaknesses are exposed, particularly by the chairman who has a reputation for 'not suffering fools gladly'.

He also feels that the directors of IT and sales and marketing are demanding more money than advisable for their functions, although he can see the strategic necessity of their requests. He resorts to more meetings than 'strictly necessary' with the man he sees as his protector and champion in what he feels is a hostile environment – the CEO – who in turn is feeling disappointed by Fred's performance and is seeking to distance himself from what he feels may have been a mistaken promotion.

The stress at work has also resulted in a less-than-happy home life. His wife is fed up with the long hours Fred works and the snappy exchanges that pass for conversations at home. Fred confesses that he is 'probably drinking more than I should' in an effort to cope with what he perceives as 'failure on all fronts'. A relatively 'straightforward' coaching assignment has revealed a lot more than the coach first envisaged.

This case study illustrates several grey areas, which leave a coach in a sticky position ethically. I will not attempt to offer an answer but suggest that coach, sponsor and client need to consider and clarify the following areas when appointing a coach.

Accountability

First, there is the question of accountability. To whom is the coach accountable – the sponsor (CEO) who has sent Fred for coaching and is, incidentally, paying the bill? Or the client, who has been honest and open with his coach? The question might be obviated by clear contracting at the start where the coach makes it clear in the initial three-way meeting what does not get fed back to the sponsor (for example personal details the client may want to keep within the coaching dyad) and what may be fed back (for example issues of progress or blocks within the business environment). It is my experience that the sophisticated buyer will usually insist that the coaching objectives are shared ('the what'), but not expect that the meat of individual sessions will be ('the how').

Confidentiality

For any coaching programme to succeed, confidentiality is a given. This means not disclosing details of the sessions. Some sponsors might attempt to bypass the issue by phoning for feedback. How much is disclosed is then between the coach and his or her conscience. Ethically, the coach is in a spot. Ideally, coach and client should be in agreement about what is fed back to the organisation and, for the sake of transparency, the coach might choose to copy the client in on any written report or formally agree the content of a verbal one. The coach might also feel that it is in Fred's interests to communicate clearly with his sponsor within the organisation about progress in achieving targets, on the grounds that any coaching programme is likely to be a greater success if it is supported by the systems within the company. In this case, that consists of Fred's team, his colleagues and his boss.

The Expertise of the Coach

The case also highlights issues around the expertise of the coach. I suggest that most readers would expect the coach to see Fred's drinking as part of a larger response to the stress he is under. If the coach is trained in this area, he may well, with Fred's assent, work with him on this. If they agree that it is not within the coach's competence to help Fred with this problem, the coach may refer him to an outside agency.

The important issue is the coach's recognition of those areas outside his own competence. While alcohol misuse is an obvious area to point to, it is less obvious if the area outside the coach's expertise is a business process – for example a merger or management of a global change programme. What is the ethical responsibility of the coach in such cases? The ethical dilemma is the same. A strong coach, in my view, is one who 'knows what he or she doesn't know' and has a strong enough ego to admit it. This is good role modelling for the client (that is, 'you don't have to know about everything – you could look for a person who can help'). The client will respect a coach who says 'I can't do that' rather than one who makes claims for expertise that are unwarranted.

Professional Development

The personal qualifications of the aspiring coach should include business expertise coupled with an attitude of mind that is enquiring and eager for further learning. Knowledge of systems theory, organisational psychology and the way adults learn and change (and the processes which obstruct learning) is also necessary if the coach is to help foster growth in a client. A qualification in clinical psychology (that is, the application of psychological enquiry to the one-to-one process) or psychotherapy denotes a level of training, although not necessarily a level of practice. Coaching and counselling or psychotherapy are different professional disciplines, but a coach with training in one of the therapies may well be able to use that perspective to throw useful light on a personal or business dynamic.

In Fred's case, the coach may well feel able, by virtue of his or her business experience, to help him negotiate the minefield of conflictual relationships which surround his situation in the company. However, while business expertise is important, it is not the only qualification needed. It is also important to know how to share that experience without directing, training or setting oneself up as the 'fount of all wisdom', implying, as it does, that the client has only to sit at one's feet for long enough and he or she will acquire wisdom by some kind of osmosis. For, if one acts on this basis, a client learns only that others have more knowledge than he or she. It is my considered opinion that the object of development coaching is to help the client to 'learn how to learn'. To achieve this, the coach needs to develop skills closest to those taught in counselling courses.

While development coaches are not offering therapy, they are working in the domain of interpersonal relationships. Indeed, I would argue that the coaching relationship, and the adept handling of it, is the vehicle by which the development coaching and learning may be owned by the client and ultimately, therefore, be used by the client independently of the coach. This implies that good coaches coach themselves into redundancy. This has two implications that merit some thought: that the coach should ensure that he or she maintains an objective professionalism in both the coaching relationship and when negotiating the length of the contract and its termination.

Supervision

First, I think it naïve at best, and dangerous at worst, if the coaching relationship is not supervised by another professional with some psychological expertise. That person is there to ensure the best interests of the client and the coach. For the client, the supervisor may be said to take on the 'grandparent' role – a kind of benign oversight of the process to check that important areas are not ignored or missed. For the coach, the role is a consultative one that also focuses on the development of the coach. The areas where most growth and learning may take place are likely to be those areas most difficult for the client, and therefore for the coach in relation to the client, to approach. This often leaves the coach feeling 'stuck' in a programme. Supervision assists by exploring with the coach what that 'stuckness' may be about and thus helping the process to move on. Supervision is a facilitating process that, at its best, promotes the coach's learning and development (and may result in recommendations for further training as a part of a continuing professional development process). At the least, it ensures that the coach is not tempted to stray into areas outside his or her expertise – whether that be of a personal nature (for example there may be a need for some professional therapy if a client deems it appropriate) or of a business nature where it may be appropriate to refer to another source of expertise. Either way, supervision operates in the service of both client and coach.

Ending of the Coaching Contract

The second implication concerns the length of a coaching relationship and ending it so as to maximise the usefulness of the work to the client. It is incumbent upon the coach to define clearly the length of the coaching programme in the contracting stage of the process. For a client who has specific short-term needs, the programme may be different to that envisaged for a development programme. Development takes time and therefore a typical coaching programme is a year. The coach is immediately in an ethical dilemma.

Fred has, in the course of a year, tackled his alcohol difficulty (with outside help), looked at his assertiveness (and now has more of an 'adult-to-adult' relationship with his chairman and the IT and sales directors) and has seen how his need to stay in control led to an impossible relationship with his chief accountant. He has managed to negotiate areas of control which leave more people empowered and, in tandem with this, has used the time released from 'controlling' his team to raise his nose from the grindstone and look at the long-term needs of the company. He is gently negotiating with his CEO how this might be done. And now his coaching programme is at its end.

Here is a moral and ethical dilemma for his coach who may well have some anxiety, unexplored in supervision, about how well Fred may cope without the regular meetings of the coaching partnership. And yet, the whole raison d'être of coaching is that the coach enables the client to 'learn how to learn'. At this point, it is probably inevitable that having worked closely with the client, the coach is finding it as hard as Fred to let go. They share the same success. Saying goodbye is hard and it also makes good commercial sense to the coach that the programme be extended. As the CEO is happy with the changes in the way Fred operates and Fred is enjoying his role as he never thought possible without the intervention of the coach, it is tempting to continue. Ethically, is this a sound decision?

I would suggest that the idea of continuing is the easy option for coach, client and sponsor. The alternative, much more difficult for all to negotiate, is that there is a termination of the relationship and an intrinsic part of this is that the coaching dyad takes stock of what learning has taken place, how that has happened (so the process can be transferred to new and different learning situations), what has been achieved and what still needs to be worked on. A follow-up session might then be agreed to check on progress so far and to take account of difficulties and successes. From that, a new coaching agenda may be negotiated or there may be a decision to have a further follow-up session or to terminate the relationship. If a client is to 'learn how to learn', then the client has to have a real opportunity to take stock of what has been learnt and to see how he or she copes on his or her own without the coach. It may then be possible to judge what has been internalised and thus has truly become the client's own learning.

This is a difficult area for all concerned, not least because it involves negotiating loss. It is hard for coaches because they inevitably have an attachment to the client and for clients because they have an attachment to their coach. However, it is an ethical way to proceed which allows true growth for both, and may well have the spin-off that the sponsor sees the ethical basis of the coaching and will have confidence in making further referrals.

Conclusion

This contribution will not have laid down rules or regulations, nor does it claim to deal with all the ethical dilemmas that are part of any coaching relationship. Hopefully, it has given some flavour of those issues the new profession of development coaching should consider to inform its professional practice. It might have made you think differently about how you approach a coaching assignment and given you some questions to ask – whether as purchaser, consumer or would-be coach.

CHAPTER 9

Training for Development Coaches

Myles Downey, The School of Coaching

Introduction

I have not yet met a child who has declared 'when I grow up I want to be an executive coach'. Most people entering the discipline of executive coaching (or what has been termed in this book, 'development coaching') are commencing on a second or third career and will either have had exposure to one of the allied disciplines (psychology and so on) mentioned throughout this book or will be from the business world itself, intent on sharing their wisdom and experience. That it is a second or third career for most people is perhaps the single greatest shaping force on the current state of the provision of training and development activities. Most of these people have gone through extensive training in the past and do not, rightly or wrongly, feel the need for more. Hence the current reality is that there is not very much available for people to help them to become coaches that is formal and organised.

The training and development of coaches is something that I have been involved in for almost 15 years, initially in a small consulting firm and latterly with The School of Coaching in the UK. I say this for two reasons. One, in effect, to present my credentials and two, more importantly, to declare my interests and prejudices; the School has a particular approach to the training and development of coaches and a particular understanding of coaching that is not commonly held.

That out of the way, let me briefly say what I intend covering in this chapter. We start with an overview of what is currently available to people wishing to be trained as executive coaches. This is important as it gives some insight into how the training of coaches might develop. Then we move to what I believe is central to training and developing coaches. This is broken into two parts: the content (*what* people need to learn) and the process (*how* they might best learn that). These borrow heavily from my experiences with the School. The final part of this chapter draws some conclusions and looks to the future of developing coaches.

I imagine that some of the notions I have included here will provoke questions. I hope so because conversation and discussion is essential. And what follows is just one person's contribution to the debate.

What's Currently Available

As you might imagine in an emerging profession, there is not much training and development available to the individual wishing to become a coach. You will find very little that is formal and organised. A brief overview reveals three loose categories of training and development activities:

- apprenticeship in a firm that provides coaching services

- training in an allied discipline

- engagement with one of the few organisations offering training in coaching

Apprenticeship in a Firm Providing Coaching Services

There is a growing number of organisations that offer executive coaching. Those that have been involved for the longest have induction and training programmes designed to support novices through the development phases to the point where they are contributing members of staff. These programmes are typically developed within the organisation, without much reference to what might be happening in other parts of the sector, and are concerned with passing on best practice from one generation to the next. Given that most of the organisations offering executive coaching are still relatively small and the pressure to generate income so great, it is almost always the case that the novice does not get all the attention that might be desirable and often gets pushed before the client prematurely. Nevertheless, I think it is fair to say that, to date, this has been the most effective route to becoming a professional coach.

Training in an Allied Discipline

Many of those now operating as coaches have taken a sideways step from an allied discipline such as psychology or psychotherapy. In this category, I also include other approaches that are less recognised, such as neuro-linguistic programming, transformational technology and The Inner Game. These disciplines have much to offer to the executive coach. But a word of warning: none of these disciplines *is* coaching. I say this because many appear to believe that their approach is coaching while the original models and approaches were developed with a different intent to coaching.

That said, a strong background in the disciplines mentioned above, and others, should provide a sound foundation for developing as a coach, for many of the skills are directly transferable. More than that, the original discipline may add value to the coaching; for example, a psychologist or psychotherapist will recognise much more quickly when an individual has 'deeper' needs that cannot be met by coaching.

Formal Programmes

Formal programmes are very few. This is not surprising as the market is still so small. These are programmes offered by organisations that are aimed at developing coaches or coaching skills on a commercial basis. In a few cases, the organisations have developed relationships with universities and other organisational establishments who provide various forms of accreditation. What is on offer is very broad in terms of quality and in terms of programme duration, which can be anything from two days to a year. In almost all of these cases the shape of the programme is dictated much more by what the providers believe the market will buy and much less by what is required to develop a competent coach.

Within each of these categories you will find varying degrees of professionalism, understanding of the topic and associated issues, and comprehensiveness in the training. However, as the profession emerges, there will be increasing need for consistency and quality in the training process. The next two parts describe what I believe to be the key elements of an effective process for developing competent coaches.

A Suggested Training Model

The Process

My instinct is to describe *what* might be learned before I describe *how* it might be learned. But because coaching is, to quote Tim Gallwey, author of *The Inner Game of Work*, 'an art that must be learned mostly from experience',[1] I will describe the process first. There is an inherent integrity in this in that a programme in which the process has precedence – comes first – is much more likely to meet the real needs of the participants and more accurately reflects the nature of non-directive coaching.

The most effective training programmes, I believe, should have three phases:

- Training
- Apprenticeship
- Supervision

Before describing these phases, I would like to flag up the notion of pre-qualification; that it is worth putting candidates through an assessment process prior to the development programme itself. This should ensure that there is a real understanding of candidates' needs and the likelihood of their success in the programme.

Training

Despite my preference towards a non-directive style in the early part of the development programme, there is a place for something a little more directive. Experience does suggest that there are some models and practices that are particularly useful and that can be quickly assimilated. However, the sooner a return to following the interest of the participant, the better. In this phase, the trainer might think of him or herself as a guide more then anything else. This implies that the guide has been through the territory before and therefore has some useful information and experience, but that the exact path is of the participants' choosing.

The purpose of the training phase is to give the participant the core models (for instance, the GROW model) and to develop the core skills, such as listening and asking questions, so that they can begin to coach others. A typical approach at the School is to describe a model or skill and then demonstrate it. The participants then practise the model or skill with each other and receive feedback from the programme leader and their colleagues. I refer back to the Gallwey quote above; people learn coaching by doing it and 80% of any programme should be focused on practice.

At the School we advocate starting with 'practice clients'; these are people who have a real need and desire to be coached but who understand that the coach is in training – the nearest thing to a 'safe environment' in the real world. This is a marvellous technique for accelerating learning and meeting the issues that the 'real world' throws up before actually being exposed to paying clients.

Apprenticeship

There may not be a very significant distinction between this phase and the next, supervision, in terms of practice. In both cases, the coach is delivering coaching, possibly with paying clients. But, in the apprenticeship phase, it is clearly acknowledged that the coach is still learning, typically in the care of a more experienced coach and mentor. This is a more active and structured relationship than supervision with a lot of attention focused on thinking through meetings, and so on, in advance (supervision tends to be more concerned with learning from events that have occurred). In this phase, the trainee coach also learns the consulting skills involved in delivering value to the client and account/client management skills.

Supervision

In a way, this is beyond the confines of my particular chapter in this book. Supervision is an ongoing process beginning in the apprenticeship phase and continuing throughout the professional life of the coach. The purpose of supervision, which I have defined elsewhere, is 'to ensure that the best interests of the Coachee and the Client are protected and to provide educative and restorative support to the Coach'.[2] Supervision is focused on three parties and the relationships between them: the person being coached, the organisation and the coach.

Table 9.1 Development coaching skill sets		
Skill Sets	**Intent**	**Specific Skills**
Generating understanding/ raising awareness	To help coachees understand themselves/their situation more fully so that they can make better decisions	Listening in order to understand Asking questions to clarify Repetition, paraphrasing and summarising
Adding	To make available to the coachee the coach's wisdom, insight, intelligence, observations, intuition and experience	Giving feedback Making suggestions Giving advice
Managing self	To ensure that the impact of coach's needs and preconceptions on the coachee are minimised To maximise one's own performance as coach	Self-awareness Boundary awareness Transparency Clarifying intent Entering 'flow'/'Self Two'
Building relationship	To create an environment in which the coachee feels safe and unjudged	Generating understanding (as above) Creating a contract
Understanding organisational context	To ensure that the coaching engagement meets the client's needs	Generating understanding (as above) Hypothesising/testing hypotheses

The Content

The core areas of content for exploration are by no means unique to coaching; it is only when they are pulled together in the service of another person's performance, learning and enjoyment that they equate to coaching.

I have grouped these areas as specific skill sets (see Table 9.1), shown in the first column. In the third column, I have listed the specific skills in each set. The middle column is entitled 'intent' and, by this, I mean the purpose or aim of the coach when deploying one or more of the skills. As a coach, understanding one's own 'intent' in any moment of coaching is a key component of becoming more effective. There is not the space in this chapter to go into all the distinctions in the chart but there are some that I would like to draw out.

Generating Understanding/Raising Awareness

Intent: to help coachees understand themselves/their situation more fully so that they can make better decisions. The primary function of the coach is to understand, not to solve, fix, heal, make better or be wise – to under-stand. The magic is that it is in that moment of understanding that the coachees themselves understand for themselves, become more aware and are then in a position to make better decisions and choices than they would have done anyway. This is how coaching is profoundly simple and simply profound. But most of us struggle to get above our own agenda and want to be seen to be making a difference.

Adding

Intent: To make available to the coachee the coach's wisdom, insight, intelligence, observations, intuition and experience. There are occasions in coaching – and always fewer than you think – where the coach has some-thing of value to add. This set of skills is concerned with making that available to coachees in such a way that they can choose whether or not to include the 'value added' in their understanding, leaving them free again to make their own choice.

Managing Self

This comes in two parts:

1. *Intent:* To minimise the impact of the coach's needs, preconceptions, judgements, and so on, on the coachee. I believe that it is impossible – and perhaps not entirely desirable – for a coach to be completely non-directive. So one part of managing oneself as a coach is to be able to identify one's own 'stuff' and to deal with it appropriately. 'Stuff' may take the form of notions and judgements that are not relevant to the coachee. And then there will be 'stuff' that is relevant. Distinguishing one from the other is clearly critical. I have also included in Table 9.1 the notion of 'boundary awareness'. There are a number of boundaries that are important to be aware of in coaching, including personal/profes-sional, coaching/counselling/therapy, in your depth/out of your depth. This last one is important, particularly when a topic of discussion has an emotional overtone. The question for the coach here is whether the coach can maintain his or her equilibrium, judgement and distance. If you are in your depth, you can continue coaching; if not, you need to decide one of two things: whether to take the issue to supervision and/or whether you need to find alternative support for the coachee.

2. *Intent:* To maximise one's own performance as a coach. There is a mental state that can be achieved in which one performs with excellence, where all one's faculties are available and one's sensitivity heightened. Mihaly Czikszentmihalyi, Professor of Psychology and Education at the University of Chicago, called this state 'flow' in his book, *Flow: the Psychology of Happiness*. I quote: 'in the flow state action follows upon action according to an internal logic that seems to need no conscious intervention by the actor'.[3] Tim Gallwey, mentioned earlier, in his first and seminal book *The Inner Game of Tennis* called this 'Self Two'. There is a skill in getting into this place. It is where the very best coaching happens. It is not a skill that I have found a way of 'mastering', but I am getting better at it.

A quote by Aldous Huxley captures this well: 'If you take lessons before you are well and truly co-ordinated you are merely learning another way of using yourself badly.'

Building Relationship

Intent: To create an environment in which the coachee feels safe and unjudged. Without a relationship, there is no coaching. In fact, the only real mistake that a coach can make in a coaching session is to damage the relationship. Everything else is recoverable. The relationship need not be particularly close. It needs to be a working relationship, fit for purpose. Generating a clear contract with the coachee is one critical element.

Understanding Organisational Context

Intent: To ensure that the coaching engagement meets the client's needs. I get into a lot of trouble over this one, particularly with people who come from a psychological background. It is important to distinguish between the client and the sponsoring organisation. Typically, there will be someone representing the organisation – the person who pays the bill. In, say, a psychotherapeutic relationship, he or she is usually the same person. For coaching to be successful, the organisation's needs must be met as well. A competent coach needs to have the consulting skills to be able to understand the organisational context within which the coaching engagement is taking place.

Future Developments

I thought that this final section would be the easiest to write, but it has not proven to be the case. Part of this is that the future of the training and development process is so dependent on the future of the profession of executive coaching, and I have more questions about that with each passing moment. So here are some of the questions:

■ Can coaching find its own unique identity? To take its place as a profession, I believe that coaching must find its own identity and, in so doing, distance itself from the psychological disciplines and from the ex-executive as coach (this being the provenance of the significant majority of executive coaches)

■ To what degree will demand continue to increase? As managers begin to 'get it' that their job is at least in part to coach, will that decrease or increase the need for professional executive coaching?

■ If a coaching profession emerges, will there be a demand for an association? Would such an association become a monolith, stifling debate and creativity, or would it provide a framework in which coaching could prosper? Whose interests would it serve – the profession, a small elite who got there first, the market/clients?

■ Will firms compete aggressively or co-operate where there are areas of obvious mutual interest?

It is my current hypothesis that, in the near future, there will be a steady growth in demand for coaching and that the market will become increasingly discerning in the selection of coaches. This favours the small firms that have a track record and reputation. It makes it more difficult for self-employed coaches who will have to find other ways of presenting themselves credibly if they are to survive and prosper.

One of the ways of gaining that credibility is through a recognised training programme. This suggests in turn that a small, parasitic industry will emerge that focuses on training professional coaches. The seeds of this are already visible. Those that survive in this 'sub-industry' will offer highly experiential, longer term training and support that will carry accreditation from an educational establishment such as a university or a business school.

Within those firms that are successful, training, development and supervision of their coaching staff will become a greater priority than it is currently. I say this because competition and client awareness push excellence and professional competence up the agenda and also because those firms will want to retain their best staff. Experience shows that this can be achieved in part through remuneration, but that training and development is a significant factor for most professionals.

Notes

1. W.T. Gallwey, *The Inner Game of Work* (London: Orion Business Book, 2000) p. 177.
2. *An Approach to Supervision for Practising Coaches* (The School of Coaching, 2001).
3. M. Czikszentmihalyi, *Flow: The Psychology of Happiness* (Rider).

PART IV

Emerging Trends for Professional Coaching for Leadership Development

---

In Part IV, we consider the current market for development coaching. In Chapter 10, we focus on the market from the point of view of the buyer of coaching services, and review the structure of supply and types of referral, before considering more generally emerging trends in the market for development coaching. We then briefly review pricing.

In Chapter 11, we look at the internationalisation of coaching, highlighting the impact of cross-cultural influences on coaching across national boundaries. We outline the extent to which coaching is developing globally and finally consider the implications for practice when coaching clients in a different cultural setting to the coach's own.

CHAPTER 10

The Evolving Marketplace for Development Coaching

Organisational Models of Provision

The coaching market today is evolving very rapidly and shows the following symptoms of an expanding market:

- rapidly proliferating competition (due to the obvious and expanding opportunity and low barriers to entry)
- multiplying definitions and expectations of coaching which are shaping the market (for example requiring the profession to be more rigorous about demonstrating added value)
- increasingly blurred boundaries between coaching and related services
- a changing buyer (from a relatively uninformed 'faith purchaser' to a more sophisticated and demanding one)
- the commoditisation of coaching
- a wide variation in pricing

Yet, despite these trends, as well as the wide range of supply factors that we described in Chapter 2, the same operating or organisational models for delivering development coaching have emerged as with any other service or consultancy business.

Figure 10.1 illustrates the two continua against which the main organisational models can be plotted, namely:

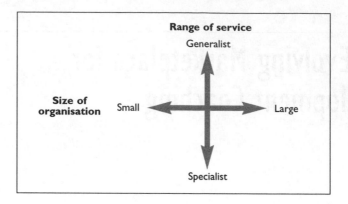

Figure 10.1 Organisational models of provision

■ *The sole trader or independent coach* – operating as a generalist or specialist

■ *Large consultancies, training companies and business schools –* offering a range of generalist and specialist services

We shall explore some of the advantages and disadvantages of these models below, from the perspective of the buyer of coaching services.

The Sole Trader or Independent Coach

Coaching is a profession in many ways ideally suited to the sole trader. The individual nature of the work means that it is largely reliant on the one-to-one relationship between coach and client, irrespective of the wider context in which the coach is operating.

Larger coaching providers claim as an advantage of their size the fact that they can offer prospective clients a wide range of possible coaches from which to choose. However, while it is important that a client 'shops around' to find a coach with whom he or she feels comfortable, this can be done equally well *between* independent coaches as *within* coaching companies.

A disadvantage of independent coaches can be their limited flexibility in working with more than one client within the same company. There are some relationships where it may be inadvisable for a coach to work with both parties (for example boss and subordinate). In these cases, an independent coach will be limited by his or her own resource, and will have to refer the additional client to another coach. It is therefore important for independent coaches to maintain a strong referral network of other coaches. A wider professional network is also important in order that the coach can refer clients for specialist services outside of his or her area of expertise (for example team facilitation, psychometric testing).

The greatest advantage of the independent coach, from the buyer's perspective, relates to pricing. Coaching involves minimal overheads. Some independent coaches do not even occupy premises, and rely upon meeting their clients at their offices or at a neutral space (paid for by the client). This is an important strategic decision for the sole trader as office costs are likely to represent 30–60% of their overheads. With or without premises, the sole trader can afford to charge less than his or her larger competitors who must support a greater cost infrastructure (although, of course, the sole trader may not wish to reflect this advantage in his or her pricing). In a business that has so far been in the introductory phase of its life cycle, pricing in the corporate market has not yet become an issue. However, we anticipate that pricing will become increasingly competitive, which will give the independent coach a significant advantage.

From the perspective of a buyer of coaching services, independent coaches may suffer from less professional support and rigour. Many coaches in the profession are not in regular, formal supervision and seem to have little source of support or challenge. Without adequate supervision and collegiate support, independent coaches can risk operating within a 'closed system'. This not only raises issues of how they gain perspective on their work with clients, but also limits their ability to generate new ideas and ways of working.

The Large Consultancy

At the other end of the size spectrum are the large consultancies, training companies and business schools who are increasingly adding coaching to their range of service offerings.

The greatest advantage of the large consultancy is in the flexibility and range of complementary expertise that is available. Size also increases the level of possible investment and the potential global reach. As more companies wish to source coaching across their international businesses, global reach will become increasingly important.

The wider resource available in the large consultancy means that there is more opportunity to use coaching as part of a more systemic intervention. For example, if two companies are merging, a large consultancy might be able to offer the following complementary interventions:

■ Strategic, process and technology advice

■ Change management guidance (for example pertaining to cultural, communication and other 'people issues')

■ Assessment and selection advice in choosing the new top management team

■ Team facilitation to develop the new top management team

■ Development coaching support to the individual members of the new top management team

■ Skills and performance coaching for the wider population

This range of offerings and flexibility has substantial advantages for the consultancy, itself. As observed by Fiona Czerniawska in her book *Management Consultancy in the 21st Century*, by employing consultants with what is often referred to as a 'T-shaped' skill set (that is, generalist business knowledge as the top of the T and specialist expertise – for example, coaching – as the bottom of the T), consultancies have:

> the flexibility to identify opportunities for new business, to change focus where a specific skill becomes redundant and – conversely – to move resources to areas of high demand. Put at its simplest, generalisation creates flexibility, and flexibility creates profits.[1]

However, as Czerniawska also comments, striking this balance between generalist and specialist skills represents a significant challenge to large consultancies:

> The pressure to specialise is mostly driven by external factors, and the pressure to generalise, by internal ones ... By contrast with generalisation – which is fundamentally driven by internal needs – the pressure of specialisation comes from external sources: the need to be able to deliver added value services and to demonstrate a differentiated positioning in the marketplace ... Clients want specialisation: consultants want to give them specialists, but cannot afford to have an organisation that is solely made up of specialists who are likely to be much less flexible than their generalist counterparts.[2]

The consultancies often attempt to respond to a need for balance between 'generalism' and 'specialism' by creating teams with a mixture of skills, experience and seniority. The 'generalists' often operate as the project managers or the 'glue' holding the specialists together (as well as providing liaison with other project teams on large engagements).

Perhaps the greatest dilemma for the large consultancy offering development coaching is how to apply the fundamental operating strategy of consulting to a development coaching model. The profitability of the large consultancies is largely based upon their ability to leverage the expensive time of their senior specialists by delegating as much of the consultancy assignment as possible to more junior, less expensive staff. But consultancies cannot do this with one-to-one development coaching work; there is no leverage to be had.

Indeed, the crucial distinction is that the nature of development coaching work is much more individually labour intensive. Depending on the practices of the development coach, face-to-face time with a client can represent as little as 60% of the total time devoted to servicing the client (not including travel).

And since development coaches need to be as experienced and skilled as their senior strategy or operational consultant counterparts, they tend to demand equally high salaries. Thus, while the underlying hourly rates described later in this chapter may initially sound attractive, the margins start to dissipate when the hidden costs of delivery are taken into account, which cannot be offset through delegating to less expensive professionals.

Therefore, the most obvious area for larger consultancies to develop into is skills and performance coaching. These kinds of coaching lend themselves better to standardisation, which in turn reduces the skills (and therefore salaries) required, as well as the cost of recruiting and training the coaches. While it might take one to two years to fully train a development coach, a consultancy can train a skills or performance coach in a considerably shorter period of time.

For all types of coaching, consultancies have a strategic 'buy or make' decision regarding how they resource specialist coaching skills. They have three main options:

■ recruit/employ specialist coaches (including through the acquisition of a specialist coaching company)

■ develop existing consultants into coaches

■ sub-contract coaching work to coaching suppliers/partners

Some consultancies actually choose to give away some of their profit margin by sub-contracting to external suppliers rather than take the risk of making the substantial investment in developing their consultants into coaches and possibly losing them if their development leads them to leave the consultancy.

The consultancies who do decide to develop an internal development coaching capability (the Organisation Development (OD) and HR specialist consultancies more than the 'Big Five') usually find that the service acts as a loss leader. While they may not make much profit on the coaching work itself, they hope to leverage the strong coaching relationship by converting it into add-on services. For example, they hope that a senior coaching client may also ask the consultancy to provide team facilitation to his or her team or group coaching for more junior staff. However, in our experience, a limitation of this strategy, in practice, is that many senior clients wish their coaching relationship to remain relatively discreet. While they may disclose that they are using a coach, they usually want the relationship kept quite private rather than blended in with a wider range of consultancy activities. It can therefore be difficult, in reality, for a large consultancy to leverage a development coaching relationship.

Some consultancies address this challenge by maintaining a 'Chinese wall' between a partner coaching the senior client and the other partner(s) managing other aspects of the engagement. For the 'Big Five' consultancies with an accounting heritage, this can be seen to constitute a variation of the requirement to maintain the traditional accounting/audit split. If managed well, there is still room within openly negotiated terms of engagement between all parties for communication to pass between the partners, thus potentially providing helpful cross-fertilisation across the project.

The other problem in managing a coaching practice within a larger consultancy is that development coaches are typically quite difficult to manage. They are often professionals who have either decided to leave line management or chosen never to enter it in the first place. The personality profile of many coaches is not conducive to being managed in a traditional hierarchy. It is no accident that they have chosen to work intimately with clients on a one-to-one basis. They usually have very high needs for autonomy, which does not necessarily make them natural team or organisational players. If a relatively loose structure and an egalitarian, open culture can be created for them within a large consultancy, they may thrive and work very creatively and collaboratively with their wider consulting colleagues. But this can be a difficult environment to create in many large consultancies, more typically characterised by adherence to tight rules and procedures as well as demanding financial targets.

An Ideal Compromise?

There is a potential compromise between the sole trader and the larger company. The small to medium-sized coaching consultancy – typically with 2 to 20 coaches – can be ideally suited to combine the flexibility, professional rigour and wider resources of a larger consultancy with the focus and professional autonomy of the sole trader. Without too large a cost base, it can also afford to charge lower fees than its larger rivals.

Types of Referral

If the above is a description of the 'supply side' of the equation, what does the 'demand side' look like? Depending on the status and structure of the human resources function within an organisation, external coaching is typically sourced by two types of buyer:

- Line managers, sourcing coaching either on behalf of a colleague (most typically a subordinate) or on their own behalf
- HR professionals acting as liaison between line management and coaching suppliers

Similarly, the budget to cover the cost of the coaching may come out of either a departmental or central HR budget.

There are two main types of development coaching referrals:

- A referral based upon an isolated *individual* intervention
- A referral based upon a wider organisational or *systemic* intervention

Individual Referrals

In the case of an individual referral, the client is referred to a professional development coach for reasons specific to him or her. No executive operates within a vacuum, but with an individual referral, the emphasis is placed primarily upon the individual's own development needs. The most common patterns of individual referral are:

- Self-referral, in which the client identifies his or her own need for career planning, a sounding board for support/advice or an aid to personal development. This may be prompted by a career transition (for example promotion or entry into a company) or interest in the idea prompted by a colleague's experience with coaching. The individual may seek out a particular coach directly or may enlist HR guidance on how to find a coach

- Proactive line management-assisted or HR-assisted referral, often in response to the identification of specific performance issues as part of a formal appraisal or development process

- Reactive response to an obvious behavioural issue jeopardising an individual's performance and progression, usually first identified by the individual's line manager and subsequently facilitated by HR

- A group of individual referrals made in the context of offering development coaching to all members of a group defined by a particular type of role or category (for example coaching provided to identified high potential leaders or all 'change agents' during a merger)

Systemic Referrals

In organisations with a strong commitment to investing in people, development coaching is increasingly being used to support systemic change initiatives (for example mergers). We believe that this is one of the greatest areas of potential growth for the executive coaching market, and indeed for the wider consultancy market as, the more integrated the use of coaching is with the business and people strategies, the greater the potential benefits are likely to be.

After all, organisations are fundamentally collections of individuals. More traditional methods of change management consulting have tended to implement changes at an organisational or group level. In these wider fora, concerns and resistance to the proposed changes are unlikely to be expressed, or even experienced (if people are not given the time or space to reflect upon what the changes will mean for them). We believe that this 'macro' approach to change programmes goes far in explaining why 70% of change programmes fail. Employees (including top management) go through the motions of change without being genuinely engaged in the process. Thus, what is effectively a charade only continues as long as there is sufficient attention on it. As soon as the consultants leave or senior management moves on to the next issue, people revert back to the way they always did things.

Due to the objective, confidential and therefore safe, nature of develop-ment coaching, a coach can surface personal concerns at an individual level and work through them so that the individual can engage more genuinely with the change process.

However, if process- and systems-based change initiatives have failed for the above reasons, people-focused initiatives in the past have suffered from the opposite dynamic – not being sufficiently aligned with the business. Even a coaching-led, and thus 'collectively individual', approach to change management must be aligned with the business context. As Martin McCall states in his book about executive development, entitled *High Flyers*:

Executive development starts with the strategic intent of the business. There must be an explicit strategy (or vision, mission statement or 'point of view')

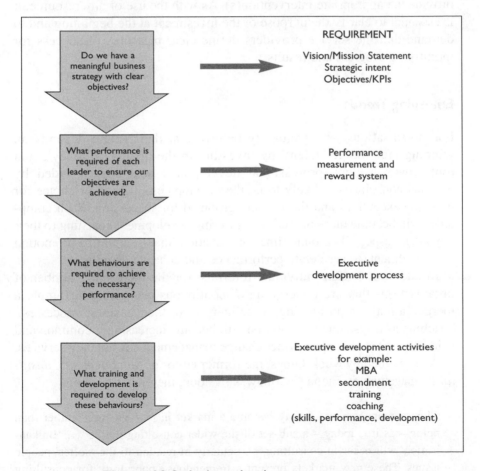

Figure 10.2 Linking development to strategy

that provides meaningful (defined as actually affecting behaviour) direction for
the company into the foreseeable future ... If a strategy cannot be elucidated,
there is no point in proceeding with executive development. There is no way to
determine what leaders need to be able to do and therefore no basis for helping
them learn how to do it.[3]

Once such a strategy has been elucidated, an integrated system should be
implemented to define the organisational performance requirements
against which individual performance and development needs are identified and which executive development is then designed to address. Figure
10.2 illustrates a framework for linking executive development activity
directly with strategic intent.

Once the required executive development is identified by such a
process, the organisation is in a position to select a consultancy service to
provide the appropriate intervention(s). As with the use of any resource, it
is essential to clarify the purpose of the investment at the beginning and to
demand that the service providers define clear measures of success for
monitoring progress and results.

Emerging Trends

For organisations who genuinely believe that their future depends on
winning the 'war for talent' by investing in the quality of today's and
tomorrow's leaders, professional development coaching provided by
external consultants is likely to be the development method of choice for
their top executives and those being groomed for succession. Such companies will become more proactive in offering development coaching to their
key talent, especially around times of transition (that is, around a promotion
or secondment) to accelerate performance and enhance learning.

In addition to such individual referrals, for the increasing number of
organisations that are undergoing *dis*continuous change (for example a
merger, a major repositioning, a realignment of their business processes),
coaching as a systemic intervention will become increasingly common and
is ideally suited to support wider change management consultancy services.

As described by Mick James, the former editor of *Management Consultancy* magazine, in Fiona Czerniawska's book, mentioned above:

Change management ... may become a market in its own right, rather than
being – as it is today – a sub-set of the wider consulting market ... 'Balkan-
isation' will occur in consulting, particularly in relation to the 'softer' people
issues. These new markets present a tremendous opportunity for consulting

firms: there are many real issues in organisational terms where consultants have barely scratched the surface.[4]

Indeed, we believe that a coaching-led change management service is well positioned to become the next generation of management consulting as clients no longer accept the 'hit and run' syndrome of much traditional consulting.

According to one practitioner:

> Co-ordinated coaching programs provide a unique catalytic agent for insti-
> tuting system-level culture change, one person at a time. This approach can
> quietly accomplish more in less time. This is because of the synergy inherent in
> combining both coach/coachee trust and the 'just-in-time' nature of the
> coaching experience with the information coordination and system overview
> that results from having multiple coaches involved. In fact, because this
> approach doesn't have high visibility, at least initially, there is less scepticism.
> Such a trust-based change process is both organic and self-organized. It builds
> on the best of the current culture even as it helps to learn, grow, and adapt posi-
> tively to current business realities.[5]

The coaching element of such consultancy engagements may include skills, performance and/or development coaching. It is also likely to include team facilitation and team coaching (as defined in Appendix 1). Box 10.1 describes a sample consultancy model to manage a coaching-led change management project.

Such increasingly integrated 'hard' and 'soft' consultancy projects will introduce even more complexity into the consultancy engagements of today (as will be illustrated in Chapter 14). Consultancies that can develop flexible methodologies to manage such integration will create a very substantial market for themselves. It is the consultancies that have tradi-tionally recruited a greater mix of hard and soft skill sets that, not surpris-ingly, seem to have the upper hand in developing this complex capability.

But even the 'Big Five' consultancies with *relatively* greater soft skills tend to possess them in 'pockets', that is, within individuals with a natural affinity for such skills and/or who have developed them during their consulting careers. These companies still have a long way to go in spreading such skills across all their consultants who will increasingly require them, no matter how 'hard' their sector or functional specialisms. Some companies are making increased use of 'internal coaches' to provide just such development. These coaches operate as coaches to clients, but are also assigned to project teams to help them develop a greater aware-ness of the people issues and the soft skills to manage them.

Box 10.1

Visioning

1. Development coach works with the chief executive to:
   - explore and articulate his or her thinking (for example vision, strategy and values)
   - express to, and test the thinking with, the Board
   - internalise a modern, authentic and individual style of leadership to model new values and behaviours to the organisation

Diagnosis

2. Consultancy conducts leadership and Board capability assessment to identify fit and gaps between vision and current reality (using a competency-based model of 'Board effectiveness')
3. Consultancy provides an holistic diagnosis (including clear 'before benchmark' against which progress can be monitored) and a tailored intervention proposal

Planning

4. Development coach works with the chief executive to plan the implementation of the vision/strategy and business plan (based on best-practice leadership principles such as empowerment with clear accountability)

Intervention

5. A team facilitator and several development coaches work with the Board, helping them to lead their areas of the business more effectively as individuals and to operate as a 'high performing team' to implement the vision/business plan
6. A team coach and several performance coaches work with project steering committees, helping them to operate as change agents through imparting excellent programme and project management disciplines
7. Skills coaches support staff in developing new competencies (for example customer and relationship management)
8. Consultancy helps to design and implement 'cascaded development process' (for example developing internal coaching capability through 'coach-the-coach' and/or mentoring schemes)

Evaluation

9. Consultancy conducts post-project evaluation against starting diagnosis/benchmark to measure added value

For the companies who do not possess the softer skill sets at all, we are likely to see a wave of strategic alliances between, and acquisitions of, specialist coaching companies over the next few years as they try to build this capability and recognise that professional coaches are already operating in the arena they wish to enter:

> The consultants of the future will probably be moving even further up the emotional value chain, and their great successes will lie in managing the emotional side of their clients' businesses. It is a change that will mean that consultants are likely to be operating closer and closer to the heart of client organisations, engaging with the latter's aspirations, emotions and politics. 'Partnership' is a fashionable word, but consulting firms have hardly started to explore the possibilities entailed.[6]

As Figure 10.3 illustrates, we are already seeing a greater convergence between the various consultancy services, such as executive search, executive coaching, strategic consulting and OD/HR consulting, all trying to deliver a solution to the increasingly important 'human capital' question.

Some of these consultancies make more natural 'bedfellows' than others. We anticipate a particularly promising future in the closer alliance between executive search consultants and development coaches as the former share a similar, earlier evolution in their service. Especially in the last one to two years, executive search companies have experienced increasing demand from their clients to widen their support from traditionally individual-based search requests to more systemic interventions, such as 'management appraisal' (also referred to as 'management audit'). Egon Zehnder, the premier senior executive search company founded in 1964,

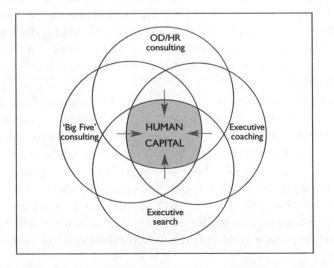

Figure 10.3 A convergence of consultancy services

pioneered this concept in the 1980s during the privatisations in Latin America when executive teams needed to address their capability to deliver in a more demanding and accountable climate. From this initial assessment service (benchmarking the executive team's competencies against other companies'), Egon Zehnder was then asked to deliver follow-on services, such as assistance with giving constructive, developmental feedback to the participating executives and the creation of development and succession plans to fill both collective and individual gaps in competency.

Thus, it could be argued, executive search companies are expanding 'downstream' (from the original impetus behind their involvement, for example to recruit a new chief executive), while executive coaching organisations are expanding 'upstream' (from their original role as support to individuals only implicitly operating in a wider organisational context).

Pricing

As in many fast-growing markets, pricing varies enormously across the coaching landscape and is also becoming more segmented. At the time of writing (April 2001), the low end, represented by personal or life coaching (described in Appendix 1) in the US, starts at around $150 per month (for approximately three or four half-an-hour telephone sessions). This rate can range up to $300–700 a month (on a similar contact basis) for very experienced coaches. Pricing in the personal market is relatively transparent. Since individuals are paying for the service out of their own pockets, they want to know what they are paying up front. Personal coaches tend to declare their prices openly, for example often including their rates on a website. This price transparency tends to keep prices low. The rapidly increasing numbers of personal coaches entering the market is also likely to depress pricing.

Skills and performance coaching, sponsored by organisations, fall somewhere in the middle of the price spectrum. Since these types of coaching are more predictable by nature, they are typically packaged into a number of sessions or hours, for example $3,000 for one-to-one presentation skills training, involving five two-hour sessions. When the type of expertise involved is very specialist or valuable (for example media training for chief executives by experienced journalists), pricing can rise substantially. The less packaged arrangements for performance coaching will fall into a similar pricing pattern as described below for development coaching.

Professional development coaching represents the high end of pricing. Pricing in this market is much less transparent and is based upon a wide range of variables. Sole traders, who do not have to support the cost of high overheads and infrastructure involved in a larger company, tend to charge the least and base their rates on a traditional consultancy 'day rate', typically $2,000–4,000. Consultancies offering a wider range of services alongside of coaching often incorporate the coaching element into the project's overall cost (although typically based upon an underlying daily or hourly rate). Specialist boutiques offering primarily coaching charge on a wide range of bases, including:

- Flat rate for unlimited support over a defined period of time, for example $20,000 for a year's unlimited support

- Flat rate for coaching over a defined period of time, involving a set number of meetings, for example $12,000 for ten two-hour meetings over six months

- Rate for a year's limited or unlimited coaching based upon a percentage of the client's remuneration, for example 15% of an executive's $200,000 salary equates to $30,000 for a year's support

- A day rate, from which the coach estimates he or she will be able to deliver a certain number of sessions, for example $3,500 a day equates to $500 an hour based upon a seven-hour day (although travel or other 'behind the scenes' preparation activities may be included)

- An hourly rate, for example 20 one-and-a-half-hour coaching sessions at $750 an hour equals $22,500; this is the most transparent basis of costing, but can seem deceptively high if judged only upon 'face-to-face' time (that is, not taking into account preparation time, writing notes after sessions, ad hoc contact with clients – all of which can add up to an additional 30% of time spent by the coach)

- Results-based, for example $10,000 to learn one or more specific skills and transfer the skill(s) to the work setting in a demonstrable way

Another variable is whether the quoted price includes possible extras (for example initial assessment or profiling, psychometric testing).

With such wide variation in pricing and the terms of pricing, it is difficult to estimate current average pricing of professional development coaching in any meaningful way. However, it is clearly important for the prospective buyer of all coaching services to enquire about how much he or she will be paying and on what basis.

Summary

We have reviewed in this chapter how the market is currently structured and the fit between coaching and larger consultancies. We suggest a buyer, when deciding where to buy coaching services, balance wider resourcing considerations against those of flexibility and professional rigour found in the smaller coaching concerns. We have pointed to the issues to be taken into account when considering the use of coaching to support systemic change, and suggested that there may be substantial growth in the use of coaching for this application. Finally, we have given an overview of prices charged in the coaching market as a whole.

Notes

1. F. Czerniawska, *Management Consultancy in the 21st Century* (London: Macmillan Business – now Palgrave, 1999) p. 83.
2. Ibid., pp. 84, 85.
3. M.W. McCall Jr., *High Flyers: Developing the Next Generation of Leaders* (Boston: Harvard Business School Press, 1998) p. 97.
4. F. Czerniawska, *Management Consultancy in the 21st Century* (London: Macmillan Business – now Palgrave, 1999) p. 163.
5. L. J. Marshall, 'Coaching for Culture Change', *Executive Excellence*, March 2000.
6. E. Oliver in F. Czerniawska (ed.), *Management Consultancy in the 21st Century* (London: Macmillan Business – now Palgrave, 1999) p. 169.

CHAPTER 11

The Internationalisation of Coaching

As we described in Chapter 2, a combination of supply and demand factors throughout the late 1980s and early 1990s led to an increasingly rapid proliferation of coaching in the US and UK. Since the mid-1990s, the pace of this expansion has accelerated sharply and extended beyond its Anglo-Saxon origins. Indeed, the internationalisation of coaching has emerged as a major trend in the market that we expect to continue.

The size of the global executive coaching market is currently impossible to estimate with any confidence. This is due to several factors:

- the substantial inconsistency in definitions

- the fact that so many companies claim to offer coaching as one element of an integrated consultancy service (as described in the last chapter), so it gets further mixed and confused

- the lack of a centralised source of estimates (that is, even HR departments rarely have a true picture of the use of coaching within their own organisations because of so much self-sponsorship)

Irrespective of the precise market size, as coaching is clearly increasingly crossing national boundaries, there seem to be three interesting issues to consider with regard to coaching in an international context:

1. Cross-cultural considerations

2. The effects of globalisation on coaching

3. Coaching across cultures in practice

Cross-cultural Considerations

Many cross-cultural specialists have warned against the perils of trans-planting business practices from one culture to another without sufficient attention and tailoring to suit substantially and enduringly different cultural norms. The US, in particular, has often been accused of cultural insensitivity and the presumption that other cultures wish to transact business in the 'American way'.

Academics, such as Geert Hofstede and Fons Trompenaars, have studied national cultural variations and their effect on how business is transacted in different countries. Hofstede has suggested that, while the principles of leadership, motivation and decision-making may be almost universally applicable, their success depends upon the ability of managers to adapt to local culture. In a seminal study in 1980, he considered four dimensions of culture, formulating a model that has since emerged as a standard method of comparing cultures:

- The extent to which people accept an unequal distribution of power

- The extent to which people try to avoid uncertainty

- The extent to which people stress individualism over collectivism

- The extent to which people value material goods over quality of life[1]

Such studies seem to have implications for whether the concept of coaching is likely to successfully travel across national boundaries. For example, in his book, *Riding the Waves of Culture*, Fons Trompenaars posits that even:

> the notion of human-resource management is difficult to translate to other cultures, coming as it does from a typically Anglo-Saxon doctrine. It borrows from economics the idea that human beings are 'resources' like physical and monetary resources. It tends to assume almost unlimited capacities for individual development. In countries without these beliefs, this concept is hard to grasp and unpopular once it is understood.[2]

However, if Hofstede and Trompenaars warn against the naïve transplantation of Anglo-Saxon management doctrine to other countries, the Canadian academic, Nancy Adler, points to a universal leadership challenge that development coaching is arguably ideally positioned to address. Issues related to multiculturalism present an increasingly recognised additional dimension to the challenges to leaders managing across borders today. In her book, *International Dimensions of Organizational Behavior*, Adler argues that:

> Effective styles of management vary among cultures. Whereas managers in all countries must lead, motivate, and make decisions, the way in which they approach these managerial behaviors is, in part, determined by their own cultural background and that of the work force. Far from learning only one way to lead, motivate, and decide, managers working across cultures must be flexible enough to adapt to each particular situation and each particular country. In moving from domestic to international management, leaders must develop a wider range of thinking patterns and behaviors along with the ability to select the pattern best suited to the particular situation. Effective international managers must be chameleons capable of acting in many ways, not experts rigidly adhering to one approach.[3]

Yet, even if development coaching may be well suited to developing skills in cultural flexibility, there are some cautionary notes for those acting as business consultants and coaches to international leaders. Charles Hampden-Turner and Fons Trompenaars argue in *The Seven Cultures of Capitalism* that 'the whole consultant culture is American; the very idea of sending a wise individual to mend a group is an individualistic concept'.[4] While professional development coaches do not attempt to '*mend* a group', or even an individual, the one-to-one coaching process does have as its premise a focus upon an individual and his or her development. Thus, it is most important for development coaches working outside of their own culture to be aware of their own cultural biases, and how these biases may be built into the very nature of their approach. Hofstede advises those in development roles to be aware that:

> Management practices in a country are culturally dependent, and what works in one country does not necessarily work in another. However not only the managers are human and children of their culture; the management teachers, the people who wrote and still write theories and create management concepts, are also human and constrained by the cultural environment in which they grew up and which they know.[5]

Hofstede cites as examples of such management concepts: 'performance appraisal systems, management by objectives, strategic management and humanization of work', all of which he describes as Anglo-Saxon inventions.[6] Considering that executive coaching at least implicitly endorses such concepts, the message from such cross-cultural experts seems to be that coaches need to be culturally sensitive when working across borders. In particular, they should expect to encounter different opinions on whether the concept of coaching, itself, is an appropriate form of leadership development (and, indeed, whether there is a value in actively 'developing' leaders at all). For example, Confucianism, a source of values and beliefs for many Chinese, teaches that people are not equal. To this day, people in China are defined by their role in society and their contribution to it. Status is influenced by relationship, which is in turn attached to implicit duties and obligations. People are viewed as relational beings, regulated by pivotal relationships that dictate an individual's obligations ('renqing') towards other people. Observance of proper relationships is essential for the smooth functioning of society. Thus, the concept of development coaching, based upon a partnership of equals, may not be compatible with Confucian values, in which a relationship between a 'wise elder' and an 'apprentice' is more common.

The Effects of Globalisation on Coaching

To balance these cautionary messages, however, one needs to appreciate another powerful dynamic at work: globalisation. Whereas each country may have historically and culturally different approaches to business, leadership and leadership development, some of these do seem to be increasingly blurring across borders, as well as within borders. Swiss Germans have historically been very different from Swiss French and Swiss Italians. Germans from Hanover are not like those from Munich. China's northern managers are different from those from the south. Yet, both *inter-* and *intra*-cultural distinctions are beginning to diminish in the wake of globalisation.

As far back as 1983, the Harvard marketing professor Theodore Levitt declared in an article in the *Harvard Business Review*, entitled 'The Globalization of Markets', that 'the world's needs and desires have been irrevocably homogenized ... different cultural preferences, national tastes and standards, and business institutions are vestiges of the past'.[7] Fifteen years after his article, Theodore Levitt has been proven visionary; international business culture is substantially more homogeneous.

Even according to one of the cautionary academics quoted earlier, globalisation is having a profound effect:

> Traditionally, corporate visions have reflected the values and goals of the society in which they were a part. Today, with the dominant presence of multinational and global firms, corporate visions are becoming transnational ... Whereas historical feuds remain nationally defined at government levels, economic pragmatism vanquishes them at a corporate level. Corporate leaders have chosen to transcend national boundaries in ways that remain outside the realm of government diplomats: if it is good for business, it is worth learning and doing.[8]

Some worry that this increasingly uniform business culture is gaining dominance over national cultures (for example ubiquitous brands such as McDonalds and Microsoft). There is also increasing concern that the multinationals wield more power than governments (for example the GM food debate in the UK and the riots at the World Trade Organization meetings in Seattle and Prague).

Whether or not these larger concerns are valid, coaching does seem to be benefiting from the globalisation of business, in particular by 'travelling' via the multinationals who increasingly act like bees cross-pollinating flowers. Large oil, banking and technology companies – to name just a few of the most global sectors – are increasingly standardising their businesses across the world, and with that, their training and development. Therefore, senior executives of a multinational corporation working in Hong Kong, New York or London, are increasingly likely to be offered the same 'development menu', of which coaching is more and more likely to be an option.

Although there has so far been less spontaneous emergence of coaching within *indigenous* organisations in non-Anglo-Saxon countries, early signs indicate that organisations within these countries are increasingly adopting similar management practices, including coaching, from multinationals operating within their countries. For example, although Belgian business culture has traditionally been conservative (and therefore not conducive to approaches like coaching), as increasing numbers of multinationals have located in Brussels, local companies are beginning to experiment with the use of coaching.

In addition, cultures *within* countries are changing. For example, the management cultures in Switzerland, France, Germany and the Netherlands increasingly represent a mix of 'old attitudes' (for example an incremental, conservative approach) and newer ones (for example greater entrepreneurialism responding to increasing international competition eating into their domestic markets). When the European Accords are implemented in early 2002, this will be accelerated since borders will be much more open and foreign management and labour will come in.

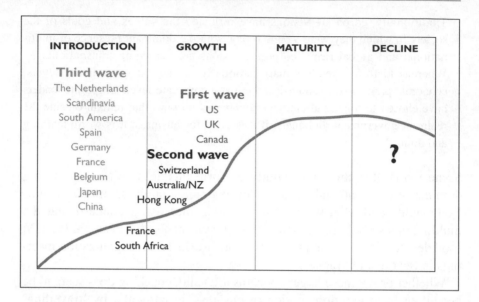

Figure 11.1 A snapshot of the current international market

During our research for the book, we have reached some hypotheses about how coaching is evolving in different parts of the world. Figure 11.1 is meant to represent a snapshot of the current international market, mapped against the traditional product life cycle model. Our analysis is very impressionistic, but we hope that it may provide a useful starting point for the reader to consider developments in his or her own country.

Coaching in Anglo-Saxon countries shows most of the signs of being established in the 'growth' phase (for example increasing demand, rapid proliferation of providers, early signs of pricing pressure, some professional endeavours to co-ordinate the 'industry'). Continental European and Asian countries seem to be in various stages of an 'introductory' phase to coaching (for example more experimental demand and supply, relatively high pricing, high diversity of offerings).

More specifically, as we described in Chapter 2, the US and the UK constituted a 'first wave' of coaching in the early 1990s. Australia and Hong Kong, often 'early adopters' of Anglo-Saxon business trends, seem to have picked up coaching next, around the mid to late 1990s. Continental Europe, Scandinavia and Asia (especially northern China) now seem to represent a 'third wave' of coaching market development, manifested by more patchy experimentation with coaching.

In Continental Europe and Asia, we speculate that the take-up in coaching, as with many Western business trends, has been slower due to the preponderance of small and medium-sized enterprises (SMEs). Whether in Germany or Taiwan, these companies, usually family run, have historically been more traditional, insular businesses. However, with increasing global competition, the more progressive ones (often driven by a younger member of the family, who has sometimes gone to do an MBA at Harvard or INSEAD and brought back a 'new toolkit') are responding by adopting more modern management styles and techniques, including coaching.

Indeed, there are a lot of common issues (for example inventory control, cash management), which managers address around the world. For example, in China managers are increasingly aware of the need to control business using Western methods. The skill in cultural management lies in understanding what are common issues and what are unique, as well as in knowing how people behave under the influence of their cultural upbringing, and in understanding why.

In some countries there are also particularly strong local forces for change in the business culture and leadership. South Africa is perhaps the best example of this. Until 1994, South African business suffered from the country's political and economic isolation. Since the free elections, foreign companies have flooded into the country, bringing with them greater domestic competition, as well as a need to compete globally. In addition, 'transformation' initiatives have required representation of the diverse population and the empowerment of 'previously disadvantaged people'. While some black South Africans had received excellent educations during apartheid, they had been deprived of practical business experience. Now that they are inhabiting leadership positions for the first time in many years, they need support in translating their strong theoretical knowledge into practical implementation and delivery. Development coaching is proving popular in supporting them in this way. However, there is a deep conviction among South Africans that they need to develop their own long-term solutions to their specific national context. Thus, their approach to leadership development and coaching is to take Anglo-Saxon models (also being introduced by multinationals returning to South Africa) and adapt them consciously for themselves.

We have observed however, that even in these growing markets, what we have defined as development coaching is still rare. In less developed markets, coaching suppliers seem to be more polarised, either coming from business/consulting or academic/psychological backgrounds, but less frequently able to offer the full range of intervention that we described in Part II. Therefore, definitions of coaching around the world are even more inconsistent than they are in the more developed US and UK markets (for example, business consultants calling themselves coaches even though their practice might be indistinguishable from advice giving and 'content consulting').

Coaching Across Cultures in Practice

Despite globalisation and its contribution to the expansion of coaching, we consider that it is still advisable for organisations and coaching providers who are trying to export coaching across national borders to be aware of the cultural considerations we described earlier. Indeed, most of the cross-cultural academics today seem to recognise both the phenomena of globalisation and the increasing homogenisation of international business cultures *and* the enduring need to respect cultural differences when working across borders. Adler represents the required balance well:

> Most organizational behavior theories have been developed in the United States by Americans. The questions they raise – 'how can I lead most effectively? How should I motivate the workforce? How can I make the best decision?' – are universal, but the solutions are culturally specific ... International managers must decide to use autocratic or democratic styles of leadership, individual- or group-oriented motivation schemes, long-term or short-term criterion for decision making. Their decisions, to be most effective and most appropriate, must depend on the particular industry, organization, individuals, and culture involved. Far from being useless, theoretical models guide the questions we ask. Only observation and analysis of the particular culture and situation involved can guide our answers.[9]

This seems wise advice for both senior executives and the coaches who work with them. However, it is a substantial challenge for people in leadership positions. A study of 21 chief executives by the Judge Institute, Anglia Business School and the Trompenaars Hampden-Turner Group in the UK, discovered that 'transcultural competence' – the capacity to integrate seemingly opposing values – was among the most important skills of the corporate leader. Trompenaars and Hampden-Turner describe the ways in which leaders can achieve this integration:

> Values are differences. They are not to be summed, but reconciled. Outstanding leaders take apparent opposites and integrate them, so that each value learns from the other, rules grow better through exceptions, and global products spread from a particular locality. These opposites might include rules and

exceptions, globalism and localism, mass markets and customised markets, universal types and regional novelties, self-interest and service to customer, individual creativity and group dynamics. Too often, a company overplays its strong suit. The leader should act as a critic of the status quo, restoring balance ... We call this capacity 'cross-cultural competence', because most of the values involved are weighted differently by different national cultures. Hence leaders must show respect for all cultures and all values if integration is to be achieved.[10]

While development coaches can provide valuable support to leaders wishing to develop such finely attuned cultural awareness, the coaches themselves must of course be informed about the cultures concerned.

In addition, the more a coach works across cultures, the less directive he or she can afford to be as it is very likely that the coach's advice or guidance will not be appropriate for the different culture. Development coaching therefore seems particularly well positioned for working across cultures because of its non-directive, non-expert philosophy. The development coach's fundamental task is to enter his or her client's frame of reference, of which national culture is just another dimension.

Indeed, one advantage to coaching in other *national* cultures is that it highlights *all* of the dimensions of culture that have influenced the client. It may thus discourage a coach from becoming complacent since he or she has to challenge all of his or her assumptions rather than presuming a similar frame of reference to that of a client within the coach's own national culture.

David Peterson, the global head of coaching at PDI, and his colleague, Mary Dee Hicks, describe several specific strategies for coaching across cultures:

Search for hidden layers: people from different cultures look at the world through different lenses. These lenses tint their values, assumptions, perceptions and relationship in ways that range from strikingly dramatic to understated. Because of these differences, coaches should assume the presence of important cultural variables that they may not understand or appreciate. Coaches need to pursue these hidden layers and bring them to the surface, both in themselves and in the people they coach.

Personalise the approach: although cultural hypotheses help coaches anticipate differences, a person's perspective cannot be predicted from what might be distinctive about their culture ... Cultural norms are aggregates across people. They can educate coaches about potentially powerful influences on people but cannot fully capture the unique constellation of characteristics that make up a given individual. Any one person from the United States, Germany, Brazil or China might be methodical and punctual, impulsive and chronically late, bold or timid ... To avoid cultural stereotypes that do not apply, a coach's ultimate objective is to understand the person as an individual and to personalize the coaching accordingly. The need to customize coaching at the individual level is supported by research from Europe and the United States, which indicates that the leading cause of people's dissatisfaction with coaching they have received is that it was impersonal. (Peterson, Uranowitz and Hicks, 1996, 1998)

Forge a Partnership: Forging a partnership is more affected by cross-cultural dynamics than any other coaching strategy. In any coaching relationship, people need to decide whether they can work constructively together. In cross-cultural settings, the potential for differences in worldviews is compounded, and the odds of failing to build sufficient trust are significantly greater ... The goal for the coach is not 'when in Rome, do as the Romans do', but rather to establish mutual cultural respect. Coaches do not exchange their view of the world for a new one. Instead, they assume 'I am not Roman, but I can learn how things are done the Roman way.' They initiate the building of cultural insights in themselves, and foster reciprocal understanding in the people they coach ... Underlying any specific relationship-building tactics, the most powerful tool for forging a partnership is the desire of the coach to understand. This motive, consistently conveyed, transcends culture.[11]

Summary

In this chapter we have described the increasing internationalisation of coaching and some of the influences of national culture upon coaching. We have discussed the importance of recognising cultural variations in coaching across national boundaries, but we have also noted the effects of globalisation in reducing the potential resistance to a development approach that originated in Anglo-Saxon business culture. We have concluded that development coaching is ideally suited to be sensitive to diversity – of all varieties – and have offered some recommendations for how to maintain this sensitivity in practising coaching in different cultures.

Notes

1. G. Hofstede, *Culture's Consequences: International Differences in Work-related Values* (Beverly Hills, CA: Sage, 1980).
2. F. Trompenaars, *Riding the Waves of Culture: Understanding Cultural Diversity in Business* (London: Nicholas Brealey, 1994), p. 2.

3. N. Adler, *International Dimensions of Organizational Behavior*, 2nd edn (Belmont, CA: Wadsworth Publishing Company, 1991) p. 5.
4. C. Hampden-Turner and F. Trompenaars, *The Seven Cultures of Capitalism: Value Systems for Creating Wealth in the United States, Britain, Japan, Germany, France, Sweden and The Netherlands* (New York: Doubleday, 1993) p. 61.
5. G. Hofstede, 'The Business of International Business is Culture', *International Business Review*, 1994, **3**(1): 7.
6. Ibid., pp. 7–8.
7. T. Levitt, 'The Globalization of Markets', *Harvard Business Review*, 1983, **61**(3): 93–6.
8. N. Adler, *International Dimensions of Organizational Behavior*, 2nd edn (Belmont, CA: Wadsworth Publishing Company, 1991) p.6.
9. Ibid., pp. 171–2.
10. Quoted in *Financial Times*, 15 January 2001, p.15.
11. M.D. Hicks and D.B. Peterson, 'Leaders Coaching Across Borders' in W.H. Mobley, M. J. Gessner, and V.J. Arnold (eds), *Advances in Global Leadership* (Stamford, CT: JAI Press, 1999) pp. 295–314.

PART V

The Future for Professional Coaching for Leadership Development

In this part, we consider the future for professional coaching for leadership development. We do this from three perspectives – a very experienced practitioner and observer of executive coaching in the UK, a large user of coaching services, and a coach and organisational development consultant (for whom coaching has the potentiality of taking consultancy forward to the next stage of its development). Our purpose is to build a picture of the forms which professional coaching for leadership development may take, the potential demand for its services and the contribution it may make towards systemic organisational change initiatives.

CHAPTER 12

A Vision for Development Coaching

Graham Alexander, Alexander Corporation

Is Coaching a Fad or Here to Stay?

Is coaching destined to be only one of the numerous fads that have washed through the business community over the years? These have often been trumpeted by consultants and training companies as the answer to the meaning of life. However, they have more often than not proved to have a very finite half-life.

In this chapter I will look into the crystal ball and attempt to envision the future. I will cover:

- the above question of whether coaching will survive

- the possible development of the coaching 'product'

- the likely evolution of coaching services and providers

- pricing probabilities

- the implications of the 'macro' trends of technology and globalisation

In terms of my credentials in attempting this, as described in Chapter 2, I bring some 20 years' perspective to bear. At the start of the 1990s, my company, The Alexander Corporation Ltd, which had been founded informally in the early 1980s and formally in 1986, was described by *The Economist* Intelligence Unit as the market leader in business coaching. My observations will therefore be informed by many years of observing (and perhaps co-leading and influencing) the evolution of the coaching industry. Together with these observations born from experience, some of the emerging trends are fairly easy to discern as one projects into the future.

The Case for Coaching

There is a case that can be powerfully made that coaching exists in a different domain to most business fads.

If one accepts the premise that human performance, learning and development are fundamental to business success, then an activity that facilitates these, it could be argued, will be a perennial business activity.

An additional argument for its longevity is that many companies have recognised that the primary area where establishment of competitive advantage is possible is in their ability to leverage the potential of their workforce. A related trend is the increasingly frenetic 'war for talent' where a business's authentic commitment to personal and professional development is a key 'must have' in the eyes of mobile employees and emerging graduates as they contemplate a future employer.

My argument, I think, is also strengthened, as has been described elsewhere in the book, by the slow initial build of business coaching and then, as results were seen, the expansion over a relatively short timescale, the proliferation through so many types of organisation, the ever-increasing number of providers and the fast-accelerating literature on the subject.

It is also interesting to note that most, in fact the overwhelming majority of, receivers of coaching are very positive about the benefits both personally and to the business. This has been relatively rare in developmental activities in the past. In most cases, with these other initiatives, there have been at least as many doubters as there are people who believe that they have obtained real personal and business value. Historically, many training and development activities, while they have often been enjoyable and a good opportunity for networking, have tended to receive very 'iffy' evaluation. There have been difficulties in terms of individuals being able to translate the training into the workplace and therefore real questioning of its fundamental usefulness. By definition, as described earlier, coaching, when effectively structured, is tailored specifically to the needs of the individual within his or her business context and is therefore 'real world' related.

Even the purchasers of development coaching, both in line management and HR departments, are in the main, positive about this addition to the developmental arsenal and its bangs for the bucks.

Indeed, we have seen over the last few years a trend in the direction of weaving coaching into the fabric of organisations. Coaching is increasingly seen as a key way that businesses can set about maximising organisational performance, learning and development and doing successful business through people. Coaching is beginning to be seen by many as a strategic imperative, rather than a 'nice-to-have' or a purely HR-driven initiative, and thus as a major contributor to competitive advantage.

On the assumption also that the professional coaching community will become ever better at proving the relationship between coaching and results, then it should be here to stay. Certainly the evidence is there from other domains such as sports or the arts. Coaching, since at least the time of the ancient Greeks, has been a fundamental part of the development of capability in sport as it has been in the worlds of music, dance and so on. It therefore seems reasonable to forecast that coaching will not disappear or be marginalised but rather have a high and important profile in the businesses of the future.

How Will the Coaching 'Product' Develop?

Since the early days, the coaching 'product' has been continually developed to be more rigorous and structured, while retaining flexibility and client centredness. What can we expect in the future?

Measurement

The great challenge in developing coaching effectiveness is to make the added value of this activity sufficiently measurable. If this is achieved, then businesses will commit significant and sufficient resources to developing or buying in this capability in a big way, rather than playing at it. They will have the assurance and reassurance that business results will follow and the investment will be rewarded.

Currently, measurability in many coaching activities is sloppy at best, and, while not impossible, is notoriously difficult, particularly in the areas of attitude, behaviour change and style, as has been found in earlier developmental approaches.

Organisations will need to become ever more effective at measuring the value of coaching. They will need to become better at linking coaching to accountabilities and deliverables, as well as to other internal systems such as competency profiles, appraisal programmes and the like. Measurability will be a major rallying cry over the short to medium term and will, indeed, differentiate between the high value-adding coaches and coaching organisations and the also-rans. The therapeutic value of one-on-one coaching has often been allowed to obfuscate the need to measure the added value as close to the bottom line as is possible. While difficult, this will need to be achieved sufficiently for major organisations to make major investments in both internal and external coaching capability.

It makes little sense for me to go to a sports coach unless there are clear goals and a real commitment on both sides to their achievement. And once contracted, there needs to be real evidence that my backhand is more consistent or the distance of my drives has lengthened. And more sets won or a lower handicap will be an even better measure of a worthwhile financial and time investment. Business coaching needs to, and will, have the same approach.

Technological Advancement

As the world becomes ever more technological, coaching will need to flex to meet these demands. My belief is that, while an increasing amount of coaching will take place remotely via telephone, Internet/e-mail or video-conferencing (a trend that is already prevalent in North America), this will never wholly replace face-to-face contact. So much is lost in a 'high-tech' without 'high-touch' relationship that coaches continue to be at their most effective and most valued when physically with the client. This face-to-face underpinning can and will, however, be increasingly supplemented by remote contact.

Demands of Globalisation

As will be argued later, it seems unlikely that a truly global coaching business will emerge. However, the potential absorption of coaching into the 'Big Five' type firms and strategic partnerships between coaching organisations in different geographies will enable a common approach to be offered to global clients.

But, as has been mentioned in Chapter 11, global providers will need to beware of an exclusively US or UK approach. It will be essential that the values, attitudes and norms of local culture are understood and accommodated. While much of coaching is about fundamental aspects of human learning and performance, the very word 'coach' means different things in different places. National cultures have greater or lesser barriers to, for example, the exposure of development needs, the embracing of the pull and push styles of coaching, the addressing of the more personal aspects of an individual's life that may well be impacting on business performance, and so on. The, thus far, largely Anglo-Saxon approach to coaching will clearly need to be superseded by culturally adapted approaches.

How Will Coaching Be Provided Within Organisations?

Given that coaching will have a significant part to play in the businesses of the future, how will this take place and be delivered?

It is likely that many businesses will continue to develop an internal capability to coach rather than exclusively use outsiders. This is, to some extent, a matter of pure economics. Additionally, while it can be argued that often an objective outsider brings enormous value, an insider always, by definition, understands more about the internal environment, the nuances of context, of culture and so on.

However, many other organisations will continue to use external providers for some or all of their coaching needs. These will include smaller organisations who will see this as a more cost effective route or they may simply lack the internal resources. Some hard-driving cultures will take the same approach as they will view the necessary coaching attitudes and skills as fundamentally different to the profiles of their managers. Finally, almost all organisations are likely to find that at the most senior levels of executive management, external providers are the only answer.

Before looking at these alternative approaches in more detail, the question is begged as to whether all organisations will include some form of coaching activity. As in all things, perhaps 'all' is too strong, but my very strong view is that the vast majority of organisations will commit to the development of some or all of their people using coaching as the enabling approach. In the same way that most sports teams, however lowly or impoverished, have a coaching component, so will most medium to large businesses (as indeed will some smaller ones).

Building Internal Capability

Building internal coaching capability involves a particular challenge in most organisations. How can they reconcile developing staff with the need to evaluate individual performance and career potential?

Much internal coaching at present is only marginally effective because the coach is also the individual's line manager. This is a fundamental challenge for managers and subordinates as the manager is, on the one hand, expected to be a coach of his or her people and, on the other, the evaluator of those people, with the power to fire, slow down or accelerate career advancement and fix compensation.

This is an unhappy conjunction at best and militates against the establishment of effective coaching relationships based on partnership, trust, openness and honesty. Most boss/subordinate relationships would not naturally carry the labels of 'supportive, yet challenging' or 'safe space'. This dilemma is endemic in the *structure* of most organisations rather than a function of a lack of emotional and intellectual maturity and sophistication on the part of the coach/manager and the coachee/subordinate.

Two Models for the Future of Internal Provision

In light of this challenge, we will see two alternative models emerge in the future. Let me call these approaches 'managers as coaches' and 'professional coaches'. They are, in some ways, diametrically opposite to each other. Which one any particular organisation will seek to execute will largely depend on the prevailing culture and particularly the 'hard-wiring' of the managers.

Hard-driving, very task-focused, unforgiving cultures and organisations, where managers are largely operational, will find it impossibly difficult to build coaching skills into their people. They will find that this is just too antithetical to type-A, 'sink or swim', 'up or out', managers. They will go either the 'professional coaches' route or use external providers.

Other organisations that are more collaborative, believe in best efforts rather than ultimate individual accountability, seek collective achievement and, where managers are significantly strategic, will take the other route. They will recruit and grow managers as coaches.

Let me describe these two models in detail.

'Professional Coaches' Model

The 'professional coaches' model that we will see in future is similar to the approach we have in some sporting contexts today; namely, for internal coaches to be employed by an organisation, but explicitly divorced from the business of management. Some organisations will invest in extremely effective coaches who will have that exclusive role and skill within the business. They will be charged with the responsibility for developing people under the guidance of the individuals themselves, their managers and the HR department. They will be responsible for both longer term development and shorter term performance enhancement.

In other words, some businesses will have what would still be a relatively novel role *within* the organisation, that is, that of internal professional performance and development coaches. Structurally it would seem to make sense that these individuals are connected to the HR department, but also crucially have a line into the operation. In addition, they will need to be seen not merely as 'HR people' but as important contributors to executional excellence and results and an integral part of the operational workforce.

'Managers as Coaches' Model

The other model, namely 'managers as coaches', is the one that many businesses have been striving to implement. Many will continue to attempt to build the capability of their managers in the realm of coaching while retaining their traditional management focus and responsibilities.

In organisations where the culture is relatively open, non-hierarchical, matrix and partnership-like, this may be partially achievable. Managers will see that, while they retain the ultimate power relationship with their subordinates, it is in their own, the business's and the employees' best interests that they develop them. Coaching will be seen as a fundamentally important methodology for achieving this.

Managers will see that eliciting the full potential of their staff and helping them to achieve their highest levels of performance is the route to them (the managers) achieving their goals. Thus, the old 'command and control' and 'tell' style of management will be seen ever more frequently as an old-fashioned and sub-optimal approach to developing human potential.

At its ultimate, in this second model, a 'coaching style' will be fundamental to the way that managers relate to their staff rather than coaching being a discrete and occasional activity. It won't be 'let's meet in two weeks' time for an hour's coaching session', but rather coaching will be a backdrop to every conversation about the day-to-day achievement of objectives – coaching as 'ground of being'.

Using External Providers

As forecast above, many organisations will continue to use external providers. This will be particularly prevalent in small organisations and in those cultures I have described as hard driving. In some cases, this will be in a co-ordinated and structured set of coaching programmes for a number of managers. In other companies, it will be left to individual managers to seek out coaches for themselves and scope the programme. Companies would be well advised to discourage this latter approach as it will be all too easy for the coachee to feel he or she is gaining value, but the organisation may not reap sufficient reward and the development activity may be out of line with the overall organisational context.

The particular area where external providers will have the most important, and in most cases an exclusive, role to play is at the most senior levels in organisations.

Professional Coaching for (Top) Leadership Development

To a greater or lesser extent, at the higher levels in all organisations, there are significant sensitivities and confidentialities, both in a corporate and personal sense. These argue against the feasibility of developing senior internal coaching relationships with a sufficiency of openness and trust to ensure effectiveness and value. It therefore seems unlikely that, in the future, an internal capability will attempt to address the coaching needs of the executive board, senior partners and, perhaps, those individuals immediately below them. Certainly there is little evidence thus far in the evolution of coaching that organisations will be able to provide internally for the coaching needs of their most senior people.

Thus external coaches will continue to have an important part to play in what this book has termed 'professional coaching for (top) leadership development'. In an ever more challenging environment, top executives will increasingly need the safety and objectivity of external coaches. These will provide the benchmarking from other organisations, the high level business understanding, the intimacy and confidentiality to enable these key executives to perform at their best, reflect on their careers and ensure lives that have an optimal balance.

As corporate governance and senior executive accountability become more rigorous (they have been far from this in the past), these external coaches will additionally need to link their work to 'hard' external measures of business and organisational performance and development. They will need to liaise more effectively with non-executive chairpersons and directors, as well as more broadly with venture capitalists, financial analysts and the financial and shareholder community.

The greater focus we have seen on stakeholder relationships in recent years should provide a structuring of coaching agendas beyond the individual senior executives' own personal perceptions and biases and thus provide a sufficient and rigorous measure of added value. All too often, thus far, senior and chief executive coaching has not had any external input, measures or benchmarking to inform the agendas.

How Will External Coaching Provision Develop?

In recent surveys of the coaching landscape, in both the UK and the US, an extremely fragmented market has been revealed. As has been described in Chapters 2 and 10, there are numerous players of all types and sizes who claim to be working in the area of coaching, as well as an increasing number of commoditised approaches to coaching via the Internet, tapes, CD-ROMs and so on.

So, from this fragmented and confusing base, how will this sector develop?

Consolidation

As we have seen above, individual coaches who work from a variety of models, mindsets and skills will continue to be sought after and provide high value to senior and other people in organisations. However, through time, as organisations demand broader and more sophisticated coaching, sole traders will either focus exclusively on senior executives or be driven down into the medium and smaller sized companies and start-ups. Those who wish to continue to serve the large and global organisations in a broad way will be forced to form more formal and structured relationships with each other. This will enable these associations of coaches to work from common models and have a common understanding of the businesses they are serving and thus a common approach.

A related trend, driven by the need to provide clearer measurability and added value and to flex coaching to the ever-changing needs of organisations, will be consolidation among coaching providers. If the specialist coaching consultancies are to survive, they will need to form informal or, more probably, formal, strategic alliances or be acquired. These alliances or mergers will be with the larger strategic and OD/HR consultancies. The coaches will provide the leadership development and executional excellence to enable the implementation of those recommendations that flow out of the strategic and high-level operational consultancy projects. This is an increasing demand from client organisations. Gone are the days when clients 'merely' wanted to be told what they ought to do with their businesses. The 'right' answer is only as good as the organisation's ability to implement the 'solutions' (that is, 'the how' rather than just 'the what') and they are seeking help on this front.

Major consultancies (for example the 'Big Five') are already more formally recognising the value of coaching and leadership development in the implementation and execution of their strategic and organisational recommendations. They will increasingly wish to provide this as a more explicit and structured part of their offerings.

However, a word of caution. The mindsets, skills and basic orientation to organisations between these alternative approaches to consultancy are so fundamentally different that these conjunctions will at best be uneasy (as will be explored in Chapter 14).

We have already seen coaching consultancies, as well as change consultancies with a significant coaching component, being absorbed into strategic and OD/HR organisations. In most cases, thus far, the coaching workforce has rapidly evaporated. The typically very different cultures and different business models have found it extremely difficult to co-exist. And, even more fundamentally, 'problem-solving' consulting and 'enabling' coaching have been found to be as different as Mars and Venus. Coaching is a fundamentally different approach to increasing organisational performance from classic problem-solving consulting. Often individuals on both sides struggle to understand their new colleagues and undervalue the work that they do and the skills and experience they have gained. A marriage that should be made in heaven has often in actuality been very painful for the individuals and very costly to the merged organisations.

So, while these mergers will continue to be attempted (the strategic justifications and financial inducements make so much sense), there will be tears. These mergers and acquisitions will have to be entered into with extreme caution and with an authentic commitment to sustained attention on how best to execute the integration. This will be necessary to ensure that the sum of the parts is more, rather than less, than pre-merger. In essence, the merged organisations will have to practise what they preach and take their own medicine to have much chance of success.

Given the inherent difficulties, it should be easier (but still not easy) for the specialist coaching consultancies to be absorbed into OD/HR consultancies where the fit will perhaps be more natural than folding coaching organisations into the strategic and 'Big Five' consultancies.

An alternative future for those specialist coaching organisations wishing to remain independent will be to form preferred supplier relationships with clients or, indeed, to provide outsourced coaching to the larger organisations. They will thus retain their autonomy but have more developed, sustainable, deeper and broader relationships with their clients. And from the client perspective, greater added value at a lower cost due to bulk discounting should be possible.

The above evolution of the coaching sector could be said to be typical developments as any market matures.

Polarised Pricing

As was described in Chapter 10, pricing in the development coaching market already varies quite widely. This trend will continue and pricing will become increasingly polarised. Commoditised, technological and small business coaching will be offered at low price points, whereas senior executive coaching will have a high (and escalating) price tag, with a very wide range in between.

In the future, much coaching will be contracted on a retainer and value-added basis to get away from the tyranny of 'time and materials' pricing with both coach and coachee conscious of 'the meter running'. This value-based way of pricing will be particularly triggered as measurement of results becomes more effective. Clients will want measurable outcomes and coaches will do what it takes to deliver this outside the strict handcuffs of numbers of hours. The depth of working relationship and the results that derive will be better indicators of efficacy than, for example, 'this coaching programme will be eight sessions of two hours'.

However, as was mentioned in Chapter 10, pricing per se (whether value or time and materials based) for coaching as it gets integrated into the larger consultancies is inherently difficult. Coaching does not naturally or easily lend itself to the leverage model that underpins so many professional service firms' business models. Much traditional consultancy incorporates a large amount of analytical-type work. Senior consultants are able to leverage fees through devolution of tasks down through hierarchical structures to be carried out by relatively inexpensive consultants.

There may be some possibility of this in coaching projects that are about developing coaching cultures and coaching capability in organisations. But in pure one-to-one coaching assignments (even where these are part of broader 'change' projects), probably the only significant work, and thus fees that can be earned, other than by the coach him or herself, will be where the coaching incorporates some sort of feedback gathering and analysis. This may be personal, team or organisational, but will be limited in scope.

There is probably no getting away from the fact that senior executive coaching is labour intensive and only predominantly deliverable through senior consultants.

Summary

In summary, 'chapter one' of the coaching in business journey is complete. Chapters two, three and beyond will see the maturing and professionalising of this still only approximately 20-year-old approach. Businesses will make major investments in coaching to increase their performance and to ensure competitive advantage. 'Developing our people' will cease to be a predictable but hollow mantra in so many organisations' mission statements, but rather become a key strategic plank in their modus operandi. Coaching will be very effectively provided from within organisations and external providers will continue to have a key role. These external providers will consolidate and form alliances among themselves and with clients. Coaching itself will sharpen, be more rigorous and more clearly measurable. It will be linked to, or be an integral part of many, if not most, consultancy engagements. Face-to-face coaching will continue, backed up ever more effectively with technology and cultural adaptation to meet global needs. In future, you will be able to pay as much or as little as you wish and can afford; but, as ever, the more you pay, the more you should get.

In short, a rosy future.

CHAPTER 13

The Organisational Sponsor's Perspective: Development Coaching in the BBC

Tony Ryan, BBC

Overview

Since 1997, executive coaching has progressively established itself as a primary individual development activity for the most senior levels of leadership in the BBC. The factors that encouraged its acceptance and growth were the dramatic changes in the broadcasting industry and the way in which the BBC responded to them. Converging technologies, increasing competition, new choices for audiences, the rigour of the internal market and the expectations on senior managers to succeed in implementing an ambitious programme of strategic change all played their part in creating a climate favourable to executive coaching.

Individual senior managers have been eager to harness coaching to help them handle increasingly complex and ambiguous tasks, and to increase their confidence in leading others. While the aims of coaching arrangements have always been specific to the individual concerned, there have been significant benefits for management teams and the culture of the organisation itself. Coaching has helped senior managers to appreciate the need for the organisation and its staff to have the capacity to *implement* strategic change, and not merely to have an intellectual understanding of it. It has gradually created a climate in which it is legitimate to acknowledge the importance of leadership and effective team working as critical success factors in a modern complex organisation.

Early Beginnings – Personal Recommendation

There is no chronicle of the beginning of executive coaching in the BBC. Energetic consultants have been good at targeting individual budget holders to undertake a wide variety of personal development activities. Some of these may have been akin to coaching, but it was unlikely to have been openly acknowledged as such.

In my view, the most significant starting point was the desire of one senior executive to provide for succession to his own position, and to bring to the BBC his experience of good practice in management development from elsewhere to help him do this. The director of finance of the day had experienced coaching in other organisations before he came to the BBC, and as a result he encouraged his potential successor to try it. It was apparently a successful experience.

Not long after this he also recommended a colleague in the executive committee to try executive coaching as a means of coping with greatly enlarged management responsibilities. This was the then chief executive of BBC Broadcast.

Both of these individual experiences were sufficiently successful for each executive in turn to recommend the coaching process selectively to members of their own teams. As the coaching cycle is relatively long, possibly up to 12 months, it took time for participation to spread. However, the number of senior managers receiving coaching inexorably grew even though it was not the norm for senior managers to communicate this openly at the time.

While personal recommendation and word of mouth were the initial stimuli for the spread of coaching, two other factors were increasingly influential. These were the deep-seated changes influencing the organisation and the broadcasting industry as a whole, and the advocacy of coaching as a key executive development tool. These factors and their impact are described below.

Forces for Change

The Digital Revolution and a Fitter BBC

The leadership of the corporation was increasingly concerned to prepare audiences, government and the staff of the corporation itself for the onslaught of new forces of change in the structure of the industry. The convergence of key technologies in broadcasting, telecommunications and

IT was accelerating, and the choices becoming available to audiences were multiplying fast.

The BBC's consultation paper in support of the renewal of its charter in 1996 was entitled 'Extending Choice in the Digital Age'. The BBC, at the time under the leadership of John (now Lord) Birt, expended much effort in trying to understand the nature and implications of the changes that the industry and its audiences would experience. Some saw Birt as a visionary in this field, and certainly, his own and the BBC's views about the future were accorded much respect in the broadcasting industry, both in the UK and abroad.

The top team made extensive use of external consultants to research, analyse and develop policy and strategy options. The work on strategy in the BBC in the second half of the 1990s would compare very favourably with any of its commercial competitors in the UK, and possibly also in the rest of the world.

New Managerial Capability Imported

But this focus on technology and competition drew the leadership to conclude that the skills to manage this future were not generally to be found within the BBC. New support functions would have to be created and existing ones upgraded and strengthened. The corporation recruited highly talented individuals for such roles as strategic planning, policy development and marketing. The functions of finance and IT grew both in size and in the calibre of incumbents. These new skills were installed both at the corporate centre and within operational departments and business units.

Strategic Plans

Key budget holders, as well as members of the board of management, were now engaged in the construction of five- and ten-year strategies, updated annually. In addition, a new focus was put on current performance through the annual performance review process. This process was onerous in its demands for detailed performance data, and consumed a great deal of managers' time at all levels. In the months leading up to its culmination at the end of the financial year, with a review between the head of a directorate and the director general, it substantially changed the nature and priorities of managerial work. Its advocates would claim that this new rigour concerning objectives, performance indicators and accountability were essential battlegrounds to be won if the BBC was to succeed in the new digital world. Also, gradually, the strategic and operational streams of business were being aligned and shaped by the 'balanced scorecard' concept.

Market Forces – Internally and Externally

Programme making had become much more complex. A more entrepreneurial approach was required. Producers had to be familiar with co-funding productions with parties outside the BBC. They faced more competition, both from other internal units and from independent producers who could now expect to secure over 25% of commissions from the BBC and ITV companies' total output.

A broader international perspective was also required to attract funding partners and to ensure the onward sales of the finished product after it had been transmitted in the UK. The BBC was discovering the power of its brand, although this brand had not been developed in a conventional business sense. It thus needed to determine how this newly discovered 'brand equity' could be leveraged to increase revenues and thus supplement the increasingly constrained funds from the licence fee.

Accountability and Discipline

Senior managers were increasingly being stretched to understand new management disciplines, to employ and use functional specialists, and to accept accountability for their actions or omissions within their own 'bailiwick'. It was no longer acceptable to claim that good management was incompatible with being a good programme maker.

New Commercial Ventures

A key feature of the competitive environment facing the BBC, which continues to shape its thinking and actions, is the pressure to find additional funding beyond the licence fee income to support both existing and new services in radio, online and TV. The creative leader in broadcasting now needs to negotiate with aggressive commercial parties on such matters as fees for on-screen talent, rights to broadcast content and co-funding for production. The agenda for business acumen has moved far beyond merely good budgetary control.

The BBC has already established successful joint ventures, such as those with Discovery and Flextech/Telewest, and has created new wholly owned subsidiaries to compete in the wider broadcasting industry, viz., BBC Resources Ltd, BBC Technology Ltd. There may be more hybrid forms of organisation as the government urges the BBC to find new ways of supplementing licence fee income.

People Management

Finally, in this period, staff surveys were introduced, which created another perspective on the performance of senior managers. Perhaps some felt that this was rather unfair as a means of judging their performance. There was, after all, so much new management business to be accomplished that also to be responsible for morale was unreasonable. Indeed, how could one be responsible for the impact of decisions made 'above'? Some may have felt that the people business should be left to personnel and the unions to look after.

Increasingly, however, individual senior managers wanted to know more about the factors that affected the morale of their teams and the potential success of their organisation. The top team took the results seriously but it was a source of puzzlement as to why leadership was not well rated. There did not seem to be a convincing explanation for the results or a plan that would improve them with any certainty. More energy was devoted to analysing and improving the staff's understanding of corporate strategy and the forces behind the technological revolution pressing in on the industry.

An Intellectual Approach

How, then, did the leadership of the BBC attempt to address this burgeoning agenda for change and new managerial capabilities? John Birt and his senior colleagues were sincere advocates of training and development for all levels of staff, and throughout this period there was a steady growth in expenditure in this field. The BBC continues to enjoy a strong reputation for its training.

Through the 'Leadership Network', senior managers benefited from contact with the 'world's best' academics, consultants and practitioners in fields such as marketing, capital investment strategy, the balanced score-card, change management and innovation. This network opportunity was extended to senior managers by invitation only and included study visits to best practice companies and exchanges with board members. It played its part in bringing new ideas and know-how to senior managers, and the learning style of network events was well received. The style was eclectic, non-prescriptive and had a strong emphasis on creativity and innovation.

From 1998, succession planning became more systematic and regular, and this focused strongly on the development needs of key individuals, both current incumbents of key positions and those thought to have the potential to rise to this level. Succession planning is further described below.

Priorities for Learning and Development

There were, however, some underlying assumptions about what were the priorities for learning and how they should be learned. Partly because of the preferences of the leadership of the BBC at the time, and partly because newly desired skills and competencies had to be found outside the BBC, there was a reliance on external consultants and business school gurus to shape the agenda for learning and skills development. The priorities for learning were such topics as finance and business management, strategy, marketing and brand management, project management and the management of technology. Although these needs were seen to be generally applicable to senior managers, there was minimal acknowledgement of the need for collective learning and knowledge sharing.

The personal development agenda was to be pursued by the individual, often veiled in confidentiality and certainly not discussed with colleagues, peers or boss. Not infrequently executive managers would ask for one-to-one teaching sessions on a subject in which they felt weak. The justification for this might be that the individual's time was very short and that this was the most efficient way to meet the need, and this was certainly so. But unwittingly, it set an example of how the senior individual was expected to learn, that is, in private, receiving exclusive attention from top academics or consultants. The learning process was seen to be an intellectual challenge. Indeed, BBC participants in business school programmes were disappointed if there was insufficient intellectual stretch in a course, and equally rated it highly if, in their opinion, there was.

Pressure on Performance

Even though the BBC is shielded from marketplace pressures because of its unique form of funding, it is not a safe haven for those who wish to resist or avoid change. As we have noted above, the drivers of change are very powerful, and the leadership of the BBC did not want only to react to change, but to be seen to initiate it in advance of others in the industry. This led to an agenda for change which was probably too demanding for the organisation, with unrealistic timescales and little acknowledgement of the need to manage change inclusively in order to implement major projects successfully.

As in other organisations in the 1990s, the manager's role became much more exposed, partly because of the workings of the BBC's internal market ('Producer's Choice'), and partly because of the over-ambitious change agenda driven from the top. It was calculated at one point that the organisation was tracking the implementation of some 600 projects. There was a formidable administrative machine tracking and reporting on performance, culminating in the annual performance review with the director general.

New, ambitious change projects led in turn to new forms of organisation, some based on a logic arising from the internal market, for example Broadcast, Production, Resources and so on, others designed to deal with new technology, for example New Media, Online and so on. Managers for these new positions were often selected on the basis of their successful track record in the traditional areas of programme making or editorial work. Some were ill-prepared for the demands of these new positions, nevertheless, they were expected to cope, and few believed that it was acceptable to say that the job was undoable or needed a radical overhaul. Failure or below par performance would be seen as the failing of the individual, not the structure of the role, and not because of lack of care or support from above. Inevitably, several senior managers in key positions left and, although the organisation had an acceptable reason for their going, such as ... 'offered a better position' ... 'to pursue a career in independent sector' ... 'early retirement', it made those who remained more cautious in accepting one of these new roles, more thoughtful about their own careers and much more open to sources of help such as external coaching.

Climate for Coaching

Thus a climate favourable to executive coaching had been established, comprising:

■ significant pressures for individual performance

■ a culture of the individual dealing with his or her own development needs and problems

■ a willingness to invest in the development of senior managers

Succession planning was broadened to evaluate the potential of the managerial talent pool in each directorate, not just for the current known organisation structure, but for the longer term strategic agenda. The information was shared between members of the executive committee, encouraging the exchange of views about future potential and raising the priority for development of the individuals who might play an important part in the future of the BBC. All those in key positions, or those with potential to advance further, were expected to have a current and appropriate personal development plan. The head of executive development was encouraged to support managers or the individual themselves to create a good personal development plan. This was done by involving management development advisers in directorates whenever appropriate.

Personal Development Plans

In working with individual senior managers on personal development plans, there were some common themes. Many had avoided formal management development activity during their careers, and indeed were suspicious of it. They were unaware of the succession planning process or what it might mean for them. They knew that some people were 'sent' to international business schools, but they knew little about them; some were critical of the expense involved in this, and some observed that it didn't seem to improve or change the manager in question. Some would welcome the invitation to go to a business school but would probably see it as a reward for good work and recognition that they were valued. Without exception, the main preoccupation was how to succeed in their current position and to deal with the kind of challenges outlined above. Long hours and concern about the lack of work–life balance were also common.

Those who had attended an executive programme at a business school were grateful for the experience. Their confidence had been raised. The mystique had been lifted from previously feared topics. Living in an international community for just four or five weeks had a major impact. It helped them to develop a perspective about the UK and the BBC, and to appreciate the BBC's potential as an international brand. They were able to measure themselves against their classmates, to take stock of their career and form friendships and networks for the future. In general, they were positive advocates of the experience to others who might be thinking of it.

However, these business school alumni made other observations that they felt should be addressed for those who might follow them. First, they felt ill-prepared for the business school experience. This was not just missing out on homework immediately prior to the class, but lacking an overall awareness of their strengths and weaknesses meant they did not get the most out of the programme. Second, on their return, they found it very difficult to apply or implement what they had learned, and so the potential benefit gradually evaporated.

It was decided to adopt executive coaching as the intervention most likely to meet these key senior management needs, viz., helping the individual to succeed in his or her role, developing a much better understanding of strengths and weaknesses as a foundation for planning personal development and helping the individual get more out of an executive development programme and to be supported in applying the learning gained from it.

To address these potential problems, management development advisers encouraged individuals to undertake the coaching process for up to a year before embarking on management training courses. General management courses at international business schools remain an important development resource for the benefits cited above by past participants. But the aim now is to enhance the individual's experience there as a result of the coaching work done in advance of the programme.

Key Issues

Evaluation

Approximately 70 senior managers have undertaken coaching with an external coach in the years 1998 to 2001. Two evaluation studies have been conducted during this time.

In 1999, the 12 members of the Broadcast senior management team who had been working with a coach were surveyed regarding their experience of coaching. The results were extremely positive, with 80% rating the effectiveness and quality of the experience as satisfied or highly satisfied. Respondents identified issues such as greater self-awareness, greater self-confidence, ability to communicate 'upwards' and 'downwards' more effectively and achieving greater buy-in from their team as key benefits to them.

Another evaluation study has recently been conducted with all those who have completed a coaching cycle. Of the 25 managers who had responded at the time of writing, all cited 'improved personal effectiveness' and 'improving leadership skills' as their aims in working with a coach. 'Developing teamwork capabilities' was also cited as an objective by 80%. Only 25% set an objective to improve their knowledge and understanding of a business topic, and in each case this was 'strategy'.

The rating of the effectiveness of coaching was positive: 80% were satisfied or highly satisfied. The most frequently cited benefits were: improved self-confidence and improved relationships, with, in descending order, team members, boss, internal customers and external customers.

Significant improvement in their leadership capabilities was claimed by 75% and in their team working capabilities by 68%. Nearly all respondents acknowledged some improvement in their knowledge and understanding of business subjects, even though they had not identified this as an objective at the outset. The subjects identified were strategy (25%), finance (6%), marketing (12%), competition (18%) and technology (6%).

All but two strongly preferred coaching as an approach to learning and improved performance in comparison to executive education at business schools.

Most made additional appreciative comments about their coach and his or her contribution to their success or survival in a difficult role or difficult business conditions. The most frequent additional comments were about helping candidates to understand their strengths and weaknesses, to reflect more both before and after taking action and to develop better working relationships with their boss and immediate team. Two respondents were disappointed that their coach was insufficiently challenging and one would have preferred a more directive approach.

Fifty per cent involved their team in the coaching process and this typically led to team workshops using a 360-degree appraisal instrument. Thirty-seven per cent had involved their boss and, without exception, had found this beneficial and helpful in achieving their development aims.

Many written comments were added to the questionnaires and almost all were positive in acknowledging the benefits of the coaching experience. Several claimed that they would not have survived in their position without the support of their coach.

Selecting Coaches

An informal survey of firms offering coaching was conducted and initially two were selected to work with the BBC. The criteria used were the experience and track record of coaching at board and senior management levels and the breadth of experience and level of 'qualification' offered by the coaches within the firm.

It was also important that the potential candidates could offer a range of coaching inputs appropriate to individual needs, and that coaches worked in a regime of supervision. Finally, it was preferable that individual coaches had experience of managerial responsibility at a senior level.

It has been the practice in the BBC to give the individual a choice of coaching partner, acknowledging that positive personal chemistry is vital to a successful coaching experience. Thus, coaching partners need to have sufficient scale to provide this.

Goals for the Coaching Contract

Coaches are asked to take an holistic approach to the development of the individual. Typically, this will involve a thorough diagnosis of the individual's preferences and strengths and weaknesses, as well as a review of the coachee's role and objectives, key organisational relationships and business processes which are significant for the individual. It is very important that the individual's boss is included in agreeing goals for the coaching experience, and, in most cases, this will lead to the boss's involvement in enabling their achievement. By the end of the cycle, the individual should have created a comprehensive development plan and put into practice new skills, capabilities and tactics.

Concerns

If the goals above are not clearly agreed, then there is a danger that the coaching relationship lacks a firm business purpose. Coachees may be too comfortable with an unchallenging mentoring relationship in the absence of input from management. Equally, if coaches overemphasise their own interests and strengths in the agenda they agree with their client, then the coachee receives unbalanced attention. Typically, too much effort is devoted to individual motivations and values, while business performance and organisational clues are missed.

Sometimes coaching is requested when a decision has already been made that the individual is failing and there is no commitment to his or her future career development within the organisation, but, regrettably, neither the individual nor the coach is aware of this. On the other hand, there are situations where a good coach should be able to help the coachee to develop greater understanding of how his or her performance is rated by his or her boss, and to became more politically aware of strategic and operational influences on the perception of his or her performance in the wider organisation.

The Future

Executive coaching will continue to be a key part of personal development for senior managers in the BBC. On balance, the advantages and benefits strongly outweigh the concerns. We will attempt to improve the contract-setting stage, including all the relevant parties so as to ensure positive outcome for both the business and the individual. Those who have completed a coaching cycle are a potential resource as mentors or coaches for future leadership development activities in the BBC.

While we have been describing coaching experiences for senior managers, the same industry and organisational pressures are being experienced by mangers at every level, and the demand for coaching support has grown rapidly. Using external coaches for such a large population is not an option for financial reasons, so the development of an internal pool of coaches has begun, and the signs are that this will be a major influence on growing organisational capability in the BBC in the years to come.

CHAPTER 14

Development Coaching in a Consulting Context

Peter Fahrenkamp, Pax Consulting

This chapter looks at the nature and current state of conventional corporate management consulting, juxtaposes shifts in both coaching and consulting to look at blending the two disciplines, and defines a new breed of consultancy service termed *personal and corporate facilitation*.

Conventional Corporate Consulting

Profit and Value

Conventional corporate consulting, as practised by large international and US-based consulting companies such as Accenture (formerly Andersen Consulting), KMPG, Ernst & Young, Deloitte Touche, and PricewaterhouseCoopers (the 'Big Five'), is a highly competitive field with a short-termist business culture at its core. The large consultancies' self-definition, coupled with their profit-driven bottom line, often conflicts with providing the highest value-added service to the client. Most consulting revenue models are either based on, or include, 'time and expenses'. This leads to a practice where the consultancy's internal measure of success is viewed as proportional to the duration of an engagement rather than the fulfilment of the client's actual needs. There are many questions as to the long-term viability of this type of model and its ability to deliver the highest value to the client in the long run. The integration of any type of coaching into traditional consulting engagements is rarely considered, and then only if it is required to progress an engagement. One could argue that a goal of coaching is to achieve the client's independence of its services, while a goal of conventional consulting is to reinforce the client's dependence on outside expertise.

Changing Identity

The increasing acceleration and compression of time in the 1990s – due to the proliferation of information technology coupled with an emerging need for more flexible and adaptive business paradigms – initiated the identity crisis of mainstream consulting. The traditional consulting expertise began to include a new breed of subject matter experts who have 'softer' skills such as communication, mediation and conflict resolution. The largest consultancy of European origin only began adding communication subject matter experts to its multinational team in 1995. The inclusion of soft skills experts on consulting teams within the larger international consultancies such as the 'Big Five' has expanded their definition of *process* consulting to now include *human* processes in addition to *business* processes. However, this development still maintains the traditional model's understanding of the consultant being the 'content expert'. Equally, although consulting interventions are of a systemic nature, the approach is generally mechanistic and formulaic and thus at odds with the nature of systems as living and changing entities.

The End of an Era

A further identity shake-up of the 'Big Five' consulting firms was caused by the Securities and Exchange Commission's (SEC) concern over the lack of auditor independence. The SEC's investigation referred to a conflict of interest as the 'Big Five' derived an increasing share of their revenues from consulting while performing audit work with the same client. In anticipation of being forced to choose between their consulting and auditing businesses by the SEC, several of the 'Big Five' began to spin-off or sell their consulting divisions over the past two years. For example, Ernst & Young sold its consulting arm to the French firm Cap Gemini, while Andersen Consulting was spun off from Arthur Andersen and now is Accenture. These newly freed consultancies are now competing in an e-commerce centric environment, which over the past few years has seen the emergence of its own breed of more flexible Internet-based consulting companies with innovative and more progressive business models.

Success: *Not* Business as Usual

The current reinvention of the conventional consulting world has questioned its definition of success. Competition in an Internet-influenced economy presented new requirements such as nimbleness, velocity and turn-on-a-dime capacities. Most of the 'Big Five's' newly emerging consulting divisions were hard pressed to stay ahead of their client's rapidly changing needs and challenges. The newly acquired (human process) skill sets such as communication, flexibility and collaboration require competencies that heretofore were part of the world of coaching. In today's fast-changing, fast-paced and insecure *e*-conomy, survival is based on the ability to collaborate with, and customise, the service offering for the client. Faced with a changing landscape and with attrition and defection from within, the conventional corporate consultancies' reinvention process reveals that they are borrowing freely from the early days of coaching. A snapshot into current day engagements continues to reveal tendencies such as experimental approaches to solutions, corporate informality, emphasis on human process expertise and psychologically savvy approaches to client issues and needs.

Coaching + Consulting = X

Blending Differences

Combining coaching and consulting into one equation introduces an entirely new conversation. The consultancies' borrowing of coaching skill sets raises a number of considerations, which juxtapose the two disciplines in a new light. While coaching has so far confined itself to individual or team-sized interventions, conventional consulting has focused on systemic interventions. However, systemic interventions are more successful when truly desired, understood and supported by *key individuals* and *key teams* within the client organisation. Equally, individual and team-sized interventions achieve higher integration and sustainable impact when supported by compatible systemic interventions. This interrelationship and apparent interdependence addresses a very important opportunity for both corporate consultants and development coaches.

Distant Cousins, Not (Yet) on Speaking Terms

The Internet age has given rise to the networked economy, where traditional corporate boundaries are dissolved, relationships with competitors are forged and new business skills are needed. Coaches are increasingly working with clients who are in the throes of these corporate changes, thus having to gain an ever-deeper systemic and corporate understanding of constantly changing systems. Meanwhile, traditional consultants have seen the need to adopt coaching skills to better serve their clients. By virtue of working with the same client, coaches and consultants have already met by proxy – and are in fact engaged in a relationship of interdependence. While significant gaps remain as each profession sticks to some of its tenets, the overlap, interdependence and cross-fertilisation of both fields are apparent enough to consider the equation *coaching + consulting = X*.

Challenges and Synergies

With coaching and consulting engagements occurring in an organisation simultaneously, change processes may occur on individual, team, business unit and enterprise levels, thus in effect blurring the lines between individual and systemic interventions. Whereas (development) coaching engagements aim for long-term and lasting change, conventional consulting engagements are designed with short-term goals in mind. The sustainability of consulting interventions is therefore enhanced by building in genuine leadership development. The consulting industry certainly has needs that may be addressed with expertise found in the coaching profession. Equally, professional coaches can discover that the consulting world offers them a new territory to grow into and apply their skills in an expanded fashion. As such, formal relationships between the worlds of coaching and consulting can emerge. Acknowledging their increasing reliance on each other's expertise, consultants and coaches *can* move beyond entrenchment in their respective worlds, resolving their conflicts and differing vantage points in order to realise their synergies.

Coaching + Consulting = Facilitation

This equation ultimately requires an understanding of coaching and consulting as a merged and enhanced discipline: *facilitation*, as defined here, borrows from coaching by viewing the relationship with the client as one of equal partnership, within which the client is the content or subject matter expert. A facilitation team provides the optimal conditions (which might include providing additional consultant-side subject matter experts) and processes necessary for the client's learning and achievement of *their* stated goals. Since the content expertise continues to reside with the client, the facilitation team's process expertise is procured to accelerate the client's decision-making processes rather than make decisions for the client. As such, a facilitation team is viewed not as an entity on which the client depends, but one which enables the client to achieve superior results faster. Unlike conventional consulting, this type of facilitation enables the client group to steer their own venture with temporary guidance from a facilitation team. And unlike individual coaching, these types of interventions with potentially large client teams or groups have systemic reach. Facilitation looks at coaching and takes a holistic approach to an organisation and its individuals. As such, it recognises that learning and learning to learn are critical to both individual and organisational development and well-being. It blends coaching and consulting by considering individual psychological profiles and behaviours, and engaging people on an emotional level *within* clearly set analytical boundaries that tie into an organisation's definition of success. As such, facilitation is a fascinating marriage of coaching and consulting, taking its content-oriented directives from the client while being precise in its process interventions on both personal and organisational levels.

Thus, the model of the marriage of *consulting* and *counselling* presented in Chapter 3 can be extended, as illustrated in Figure 14.1.

Merging the disciplines of coaching and consulting into an emerging discipline of facilitation approaches the client's needs without separating the personal from the organisational. By borrowing the best from both coaching and consulting, a new breed of service, *personal and corporate facilitation*, is defined.

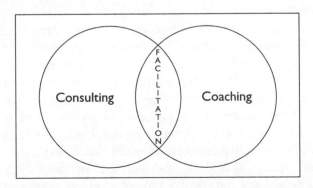

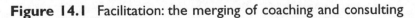

Figure 14.1 Facilitation: the merging of coaching and consulting

Personal and Corporate Facilitation

Flexible Structure, Containment, Safety and Ownership

Facilitation, as referred to here, is situated beyond the common under-standing of control-based, directive 'facilitated' events. As a new type of engagement with the client, *personal and corporate facilitation* involves key client-side stakeholders and a facilitation team who jointly and creatively co-discover, co-create and co-design a mutually agreeable outcome within a clearly defined flexible structure. I have been part of such facilitation teams since 1997 and have seen that this type of facili-tation is not just a model of what could be – it is being practised today, albeit uncommonly and with little publicity. Within this paradox of a flex-ible structure, the facilitation team, headed by a lead facilitator, is respon-sible for balancing its adaptability towards the client within required parameters to facilitate the client towards their stated goals.

The client group is responsible for defining and limiting the scope of the engagement or event, as well as ensuring that everybody needed for the decision-making processes is included. Within the bounds of a flexible structure, the facilitation team contributes to the equation by bringing itself into play with authenticity, thus providing a container for the client group's own experiences of co-designing and collaborating in previously unknown ways. This container is needed for the client's safety while being encouraged to experiment, take risks and enter experiences *authentically*. The facilitation team's credible modelling of its own authenticity encour-ages the client group to be increasingly 'real' and experience ownership within an equal partnership in which a common goal is collaboratively pursued. The creation of a safe container is further enabled by a require-ment of 'no observers' – everybody involved from the client side as well as the facilitation side is a participant with 'skin in the game'. As such, the client-side stakeholders, often large groups of up to 100 people, and the facilitation team participate as fully committed, fully present and authentic players. The creation of this safe container, in which authenticity is modelled and facilitated, is critical to the client's experience of success. At any level of recursion, facilitation of this kind engenders the client group's significant ownership of all parts of an engagement, including investment of time and money, definitions of success, the process itself and outcomes reached. Co-designed and co-owned from the start by the facilitation team and a carefully and collaboratively selected client-side sponsor team, the engagement's design is updated and adapted continuously. The targeted facilitated engagement can revolve around a central event and last from a few days to several months. It is either a stand-alone intervention (like a company off-site event) or dovetails with a long-term and overarching conventional engagement. The facilitated engagement is easily applied to individuals, teams, large cross-functional groups or entire enterprises. Since the client remains the content expert, and the facilitation team provides the expertise to facilitate a successful engagement towards the agreed-upon definition of success, the focus of the facilitated engagement can be almost anything.

Unlearning, Training and Creativity

The word facilitate, derived from the Latin word *facilis*, means *to make easy*. Due to the collaborative, creative and authentic nature of the engagements (and facilitated events tied to the engagement) mentioned here, there is a potential for unknowns, changes in course, and unpredictable outcomes in addition to the stated goals. In preparation for these circumstances, the client group may first need to unlearn – which is another form of learning – how they have always done things. In order to look at the 'old' in new ways, a new, common language among the participants may need to be created. Psychologically sophisticated methods such as making the familiar strange, the strange familiar, and making the invisible visible are helpful in order to facilitate true unlearning in short periods of time. As in (development) coaching, a psychological environment is set in which the client or client group can do their best work and learn the most. Since this environment cannot be achieved by simply *training* the client, the facilitation team must 'set the stage' and enable the client (group) to enter into a creative process in which they discover their own solutions. Inasmuch as training prepares people *against* surprise, unlearning and learning to learn prepares them *for* surprise. Training aims at final *self-definition* in terms of role and capacity. The creative processes of unlearning and learning how to learn facilitate a continuing *self-discovery* in terms of role and capacity, which is critical to true leadership development.

Transformation: Facilitating a Conversation

Learning new things and learning how to learn requires a *transformation*. One could argue that an organisation's transformation necessitates a personal transformation of its leader(s). To the degree that employees take their cues from their superiors within a hierarchy, the leaders' *public* transformation is of utmost value. Since it is much more difficult for new behaviour to 'trickle up' in a hierarchical organisation, organisational change is significantly enhanced by its leadership modelling new, desired behaviour. Thus, the success of a facilitated engagement at an enterprise level is often proportional to the level of authentic transformation experienced and displayed in public by the *real* leader – the person who carries the vision, whom others believe in and who finally endorses the decisions that are made. The effects of this authentic transformation are twofold. It raises the leader's own potential for continuous learning, for designing outcomes in a collaborative fashion and for an increased ability to tolerate, if not appreciate, ambiguity. Second, a willingness to model the desired culture and behaviours, for example, admitting in front of co-workers to being human (for example making mistakes) enables the leader's implicit or explicit statement of 'I don't know' – which engenders compassion from peers and subordinates. This is a significant event for all participants and not only increases their dedication towards achieving organisational goals, but also engenders their willingness for considered risk-taking and collaboration. Often, this is the first time that long-standing co-workers meet as real people, take risks in front of each other and truly collaborate. Thus, a *conversation* is facilitated, and personal transformation creates the possibility for organisational transformation. Clients who experience this type of facilitation often express a strong desire to have a facilitation team *permanently on site* in order to assist them continuously.

New Roles, New Skills

There are two key components supporting the client's desire for access to facilitation teams. The holistic facilitation of both the individual and the enterprise at the same time *and* the extreme 'usability' of a facilitation team – its thorough service attitude allows the client to leverage the facilitation team's skill sets for the client's own purposes. During facilitated engagements and events (as described here), a facilitator often functions as confidant and coach to the real leader, as 'go-to' person for the sponsor team and as facilitator for all participants. Attempting to fully understand the client issues, the facilitator needs to be in sync with where the client is in their process. While the client perceives the facilitator as figurehead of the facilitation team, the facilitator views him or herself as (just) one more member of the facilitation team. In order to be of true and competent service to the client, facilitation team members wear multiple hats simultaneously and their role definitions approach *personal and corporate facilitation*. People of such competence draw on a multitude of disciplines to make them as well-rounded, nimble and adept as required in order to respond to the client's needs on a multitude of levels. While the distinctions of consultant or coach are irrelevant to the self-definition of a facilitation team, its members must know exactly where their boundaries and competencies are situated. Conventional consultants, subject matter experts or coaches may all continue to play their own roles as specialists in their own domains and dovetail with a facilitated engagement. However, the (self-) definition of facilitation teams requires a completely new understanding of both their role and their skill set. The personal and corporate facilitator is consultant, coach, specialist, generalist and 'fallible human' – all in one. The facilitator temporarily and authentically *enters* the client's world empathetically, thereby facilitating the client's (and often also the real leader's) own authentic processes and transformations. This requires the facilitator to let go of controlling situations, tolerate ambiguity and be able to change course at a moment's notice. To this end, the lead facilitator is being supported by a highly competent team of *knowledge-workers* – highly skilled generalists who provide insight and execution based on tacit knowledge gained through real-time information assimilation and their previous learning activities. In a business climate increasingly real-time based, a facilitation team of this nature is equipped to parachute into a client situation and facilitate the highest quality of real-time work, while doing its utmost to enable instant change with sustainable long-term implications.

Synergies and Homogenisation

A client's appetite for having its individuals and organisation treated as holistic entities by very capable facilitation teams is significant. There is a high demand for very apt and gifted key individuals (facilitators) who are the figureheads of such personal and corporate interventions, and who serve as the single point of contact for organisational leaders to pilot them through extremely challenging and complex change processes. When a client group feels fully engaged, fully respected and fully understood by the facilitation team, the group is (psychologically speaking) *receptive* enough to be supported in overcoming their own obstacles towards achieving their desired goals. In this (psychological) *space*, a facilitation team has the opportunity to successfully demonstrate and establish patterns for learning, learning to learn and sustainability, which the client may carry over into their daily organisational life. A facilitation team applies its consultants as coaches, its coaches as consultants, its specialists as generalists and its generalists as specialists. Its members are *personal and corporate facilitators*, able to temporarily slip into any of these roles as needed. The notion of personal and corporate facilitation therefore emerges as a marriage of the worlds of consulting and coaching, and, with a homogenised skill set, as a new service line.

Limitations, Possibilities and Experience

More often than not, if the facilitated engagements or event-based, stand-alone interventions described here are driven by crisis, the solutions developed only address short to medium-term goals and the stated definition of success is rarely aligned with becoming a continuous learning organisation. However, highly creative and refined approaches to solving complex problems *can* enable the client to learn, learn how to learn and develop new, collaborative ways of working in very short periods of time. While long-term and vision-driven engagements certainly increase the capacity for lasting change, clients *can* be facilitated towards their success in all timeframes while in the process authentically experiencing that things are done differently and better results are achieved. This way of working introduces a redefinition of the consulting term engagement. An example of this can be found at one of the large international consulting firms, which has facilitated the leadership of over 200 Fortune 500 companies since mid-1996 through collaboratively designed engagements and events. I have worked with firms such as this one on over 75 facilitated engagements and events, which has furthered my own practice of personal and corporate facilitation. Using innovative, proven facilitation methodologies, these engagements and events have managed to incorporate authentic learning and learning to learn into their design. According to the leadership of over 95% of these clients, superior and lasting results have been achieved in a much shorter timeframe than previously thought possible. This remarkable client acclaim is supported not only by a mutual willingness to co-discover and co-design, but by a flexible structure of facilitation methodologies whose complexity does not lend itself to detailed delineation here. What follows is a brief overview of some elements of the methodology:

■ custom-designed work environments provide an open, flexible, and creativity-enhancing work space

- very large, rolling walls both delineate momentarily created workspaces *and* function as huge whiteboards or places to post information

- all work-related furniture is on wheels and can be reconfigured at a moment's notice to accommodate fluctuating sizes of client-side work teams in order to enhance collaboration and efficiency

- a state-of-the-art technical environment allows for rapid system development and prototyping of designs or potential solutions

- all client-generated processes and outcomes are immediately captured and rendered electronically to enable instant and ongoing visualisation and mining of valuable data

- client assignments and exercises are designed by the facilitation team to allow for parallel processing in order to compress time

- an eclectic assortment of books, toys, puzzles and interactive technologies stimulate creative thinking while also absorbing nervous energies

Thus, a psychological and physical environment is provided to facilitate creativity, support collaboration and enable focused and efficient group work. Clients have estimated that several months' worth of work have been achieved within a few days with the utilisation of these facilitation methods. In order to facilitate this accomplishment, facilitators and their teams undergo a rigorous and specific education, conducted by those few who are knowledgeable and experienced in the field of personal and corporate facilitation. Within this market, the art of facilitation has been honed to include best practices from the worlds of consulting, development coaching, psychology and continuous learning.

Industry Trends

Personal and corporate facilitation, as described here, can be expected to yield further trends and insights towards future approaches and definitions of coaching and consulting. However, the conventional consulting world's definition of success may only slowly include dynamics such as sustainability, education and learning to learn. Coaches today are facilitating their individual and team-sized clients towards greater awareness and increased capacities to learn, adapt and change within their clients' corporate whirlwind conditions. Consultants are realising their personal need to increase their own capacities in these areas, as well as the need to expand their service offerings to enable these capacities in their clients. The last few years in the business world have introduced previously unthinkable mergers of competitors and the breaking up of large single entities. This much flux suggests that the coaching and consulting professions will need to follow suit to stay ahead of a changing landscape in order to provide new breeds of service to new breeds of organisations. The realisation of the opportunity for both fields to co-evolve and cross-fertilise each other points to a solidification of the continuing emergence of a new professional service line: although *personal and corporate facilitation* is not yet well known, it is both *very* successful and fills a fertile gap in the current business landscape. From an outside perspective, *personal and corporate facilitation* is likely to be viewed as part of consulting, while the inside perspective reveals its strong allegiance to development coaching.

CHAPTER 15

An Assessment of Professional Coaching for Leadership Development

Introduction

As this book has described, while coaching and executive coaching have much longer histories, it is only in the past 20 years that the latter has cohered into a more discrete consultancy service and, especially, into what we have defined as 'professional coaching for leadership development'.

So why has this activity experienced such growth over the past two decades? Has something changed in the senior ranks of organisations to cause this phenomenon and/or has the case for coaching as a form of leadership development become more compelling? What do the answers to these questions imply for the future of executive coaching?

Our conclusion from the assessment provided in this book is that professional coaching has a major contribution to make to business because it is the first coherent consultancy service to offer a practical and rigorous method for nurturing leadership talent – arguably today's scarcest corporate resource. It is our belief that business leaders are neither born *nor* made; they are nurtured – by themselves and by others. The unique contribution that professional coaching for leadership development can make to this nurturing process is likely to continue to fuel its proliferation and ensure its sustainability as a significant consultancy service.

Further, the particular characteristics of the late 20th- and early 21st-century business environment, as we described them in the second chapter of this book (for example the diminishing of corporate and individual security, the increase in competitiveness, the acceleration of required innovation and the growing imperative for continuous organisational and individual learning), have combined to create a particularly fierce combination of environmental factors in both business and society more widely, thus posing at least partially new and significant challenges for organisations and the individuals who lead them.

No More 'Right Answers' ...

Business leaders increasingly recognise that the traditional corporate model (for example centralised, bureaucratic, hierarchical, incremental) is ill-equipped to respond to today's faster and more competitive environment. Yet, the recent experiments with a 'new economy' model (most notably in the form of the dot.coms) have experienced their own limitations, arguably by going too far in the other direction (that is, not *enough* structure, processes and systems). What seems to emerge from this picture of two failed paradigms is that there are fewer and fewer 'right answers' and more and more need for continuous learning and the organisational agility to respond to an inherently unpredictable future. According to Hamel, 'only those companies that are capable of reinventing themselves and their industry in a profound way will be around a decade hence.'[1] Hamel advises organisations to seek out their internal 'revolutionaries' as their greatest source of innovation rather than traditionally inducting employees to conform to a corporate culture, thus limiting their individual creativity.

... But Still the Same Questions

However, even revolutionaries benefit from an understanding of the past and by learning from experience. Indeed, transfer of knowledge and learning is more important than ever. Although it is necessary to continually evolve new answers to new business challenges, such answers are likely to come from the same questions that have always driven business strategy and decision making (for example why are we in business, what would our customers lose today if we went out of business, what is our market, what is our picture of the world and our market(s) in one/five/ten years?).

Another Dimension and an Intractable Issue

In addition, it is important to acknowledge that *dis*continuous change does not respond to the purely rational. There is an increasing realisation in business that the strictly rational approach has yielded most of its benefits and reached a 'point of diminishing return' with its predominant emphasis on systems and financial efficiencies.

We believe that the single most important role of business leaders today is to knit together the rational and emotional, content and process elements of their businesses. In doing this, they must address what has hitherto been perhaps the most intractable issue in business: the human dimension.

Ghoshal and Bartlett describe this primary challenge for leaders today:

> The secret lies not ... in the structures, programmes or incentives, but in a deep, genuine and unshakeable belief in the ability of the individual ... Of all the elements of the changing role of top management, it is this shift beyond systems to people that most directly and most visibly influences its day-to-day activities ... Management is, above all else, about achieving results through people. Not that there is no value to crunching numbers, analyzing trends, or restructuring activities. But these traditional responsibilities have, for too long, distracted managers from their most basic and most valuable role – being able to attract, motivate, develop, and retain individuals with scarce and valuable knowledge and skills. It is a role that is, at the same time, both enormously simple and incredibly difficult. It is that task that is central to the creation and management of the Individualized Corporation, the organization that is defining the next generation of management challenges.[2]

But perhaps the hardest issue for most leaders to face is that in addressing the human factor and the challenge of transferring experience and learning between people, they must start with themselves. For, no matter what rhetoric leaders use (for example the often criticised annual report statement that 'our people are our greatest assets') or what promises they make, what everyone around them notices is how *they* behave and whether *they* appear to be open to learning.

This focus on the leader as an individual is heightened by wider social trends in (Western) society today. Society is becoming increasingly individualised. It is characterised by personalised communication (for example mobile phones, palm pilots), personalised entertainment (for example Walkmen, virtual reality headsets) and personalised marketing (for example direct marketing campaigns based on sophisticated databases of personal buying patterns and preferences). As this societal and corporate climate places more and more emphasis on the individual, business leaders – and especially chief executives – are faced with a substantial and very personal challenge.

The Unenviable Position of the Leader

The role of corporate leader and chief executive is undeniably the most complex, demanding and risky within any organisation. The role of chief executive represents a paradox. He or she has more vested power, and therefore more influence, than any other person within the organisation (excepting, perhaps, the chairman). Yet, the corollary of this power is the substantial constraints of ultimate accountability and therefore immense personal exposure and vulnerability. In addition to the contextual challenges we have mentioned, recent trends in corporate governance, shareholder advocacy and media scrutiny have substantially increased the chief executive's personal profile and exposure; these men and women exist in a permanent spotlight.

That the pressures at the top are now extraordinary is born out by a recent study of the heads of the world's leading companies by Jeffrey Garten from Yale's School of Management. From his book based upon the study, *The Mind of the CEO*, he comments 'I believe historians will conclude that the pressures of the era have proved much greater than anything most of these leaders could surmount.'[3]

If one were to paint a picture of 'life as a chief executive', it might be characterised as:

From an external perspective:

■ an existence in the spotlight as 'corporate ambassador' with a proliferating array of stakeholders (for example the media, shareholders, the financial community, government officials, key customers, strategic partners)

■ the pressure of increasingly unrealistic demands (for example to maintain share price while also taking risks and supporting innovation)

■ a requirement to appear to 'have it all together' and be on top of everything

From an internal perspective:

■ an existence in an isolated and rarefied environment

■ an absence of true peers (within the organisation)

■ a dependence on information derived from the rest of the Board (rather than direct from others further down the hierarchy and closer to the source of the information)

■ a likelihood of receiving censored or filtered information and communication

■ a risk of distortion to one's own sense of self as a result of holding so much personal power

■ a requirement to suppress personal needs, emotions, insecurities and therefore openness and honesty about oneself (to oneself and to others)

In inhabiting such a challenging position, it is not surprising that successful leaders have often sought some form of mentoring relationship. If they have been fortunate, they have found a mentor in their chairman or another non-executive board director. If they have not enjoyed such close working relationships within their boards, they have often used external consultants or other confidantes. (Many surviving Internet start-ups have appointed 'grey-haired' senior executives or experienced venture capitalists to the Board to provide this support.)

Limited Support

Yet are these traditional means of mentoring adequately providing the support that leaders of today's businesses require?

Board Behaviour

While some boards represent 'high performing teams' and offer potential mentors to chief executives, in many instances boards' working practices have become institutionalised and ways of thinking, routine. Board meetings may often follow ritual patterns. Responsibilities may be ill-defined and inequalities of power may exist between directors which cause friction that is not addressed. Corporate politics has the potential to soak up energy and, on occasion, to spread dysfunctional behaviour. Personal egos and hidden-at-all-cost insecurities may inhibit directors from saying what they really think or feel. The key relationship between chairman and chief executive may not be ideal. Strategy may be relegated to an annual strategic *planning* process without adequate space provided for radical strategic *thinking* and innovation. (Indeed, sometimes visionary and strategic skills are absent in the boardroom). When there is insufficient external scrutiny and monitoring of what goes on 'behind closed doors', the Board becomes a closed system. Non-executive directors, intended to provide an external, challenging perspective, are then rarely fully utilised in this way. Such sub-optimal boardroom environments inhibit, rather than stimulate, learning.

Traditional Consultants

External consultants can provide the objective view required to challenge this closed system. Yet, traditional management consultants – most notably the 'Big Five' – often suffer from two particular limitations:

1. A poor ability to engender their *own* environment for learning and innovation within their organisations, which is the breeding ground of the intellectual capital and services they offer to clients. According to Czerniawska:

    > Surveys of clients' views of consultants have highlighted the extent to which the latter are perceived to: follow the latest management fad; say what clients want to hear; tell people what they already know; and have little business experience ... Consulting firms have probably spent more management time and effort worrying about 'reinventing the wheel' than they have about being innovative, because the former has a direct impact on the profitability of their firm. Consulting firms make money because they reapply their learning – and the more often they reapply it, the more money they earn – not from being innovative.[4]

2. Poor insight into the human issues. This manifests itself in several ways. The senior partners of consulting firms who manage the relationships with the Board can become embroiled in the politics themselves – not wishing to confront the thorniest human (usually relationship) issues for fear of offending their senior clients and jeopardising the contract. They can unwittingly collude with their most senior clients, advising them on how to address change with everyone *except* themselves (despite the fact that the consultants conceptually understand that 'change must start at the top'). Such poor insight with regard to the human issues extends beyond the Board. Traditional 'content consulting' usually identifies strategic, structural or technological interventions without really grappling with the human motivations that are ultimately the engine of the organisation. Even when the people issues are addressed (under 'culture change' or 'communication' initiatives), they are usually done so in a prescriptive, rational, structured way that does not allow for human complexity or offer the required conditions for adapting to change and for learning.

Perhaps not surprisingly then, consultants have, for the most part, been weak in their response to the leadership question. While the inherently sexy topic of leadership has caught the interest of the consulting sector and while there have been no shortages of opinions on what *type* or *nature* of leadership is required, there has been a notable dearth of practical advice on *how* leaders can address these issues. To some degree, this is symptomatic of the more general trend among consultants and business authors to describe the *problem* in minute detail, but who struggle to define the *solution* in anything more than superficial terms.

How Can Coaching Respond?

So how can the leader, in the unenviable position described above, support him or herself in responding to today's business challenges, and especially the 'human factor'?

We believe that, although there are no easy solutions to the leader's dilemmas, development coaching is ideally suited to provide a context for the leader to develop his or her *own* answers. Thus, the development coaching task is to create the *conditions* for learning and development which are typically lacking in a chief executive's environment and which, if provided in the way we described in Parts II and III, can facilitate a shift from the kind of 'vicious cycles' mentioned earlier to a more 'virtuous' one, as depicted in Figure 15.1.

Coaching does not offer an easy solution (for example like reading a book about leadership or attending a three-day seminar appear to). As we

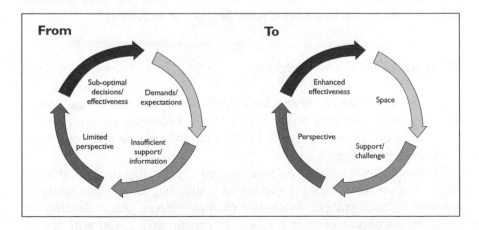

Figure 15.1 From 'vicious' to 'virtuous' performance cycles

have said, we believe that it is an inescapable truth that business leaders are neither born *nor* made; they are nurtured – by themselves and by others. However, although the term 'nurturing' denotes the slower pace of such learning, leadership development cannot afford to be too slow. Its pace must at least keep up with the pace of business and its leaders. Development coaching is ideally suited to keep step with this accelerating environment as a real-time development activity, that is, one which meets clients whenever and wherever they are – physically, intellectually *and* emotionally.

Guidance for the Prospective Client

So how should the leader who wishes to avail him or herself of such support, select a development coach? Our advice to the leader seeking a coach is to be clear about three things (which correspond to the three dimensions of coaching described in Chapter 1):

1. What you want from coaching (that is, the likely content and purpose of the agenda)

2. With whom you feel you will work well (that is, the nature of the relationship)

3. How you will test the coach's approach and quality (that is, to ensure the right process for you, and sufficient professionalism)

While you may wish to seek a coach from within an established company (for brand security), it is important to bear in mind that your decision should ultimately be based upon your view of the individual.

What You Want From Coaching

First, consider why you are seeking a coach and what kind of input this is likely to imply. You may wish to refer to the continuum we presented in Chapter 3 (reproduced in Figure 15.2) to plot where you feel you would most like support from a coach.

Depending on whether you want someone primarily to support/challenge your business thinking (acting as a sounding board) or mainly to support/challenge you personally (for example helping you to develop the effectiveness/impact of your personal leadership style), you will need a

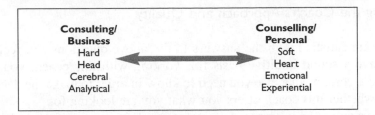

Figure 15.2 A consulting to counselling continuum of counselling

coach with different experience and skills. While most development coaches should be able to offer you support along most, or all, of the continuum, individual coaches will inevitably have greater strengths in different areas. You may wish to refer back to Chapter 6 (Table 6.1) to identify what specific knowledge, understanding and skills on the part of the coach may be implied by your particular requirements.

The Nature of the Relationship

This is an absolutely vital area to consider in selecting a coach. Only you will be able to tell with whom you feel comfortable. We strongly advise that you request an initial meeting with each potential coach and recommend meeting with at least two to make sure you have a sufficient basis of comparison.

During and after this meeting, ask yourself the following questions:

- Do you trust this person?

- Do you feel safe with her?

- Do you experience him as open and honest?

- Do you like her?

- Do you respect him?

- Do you want to spend time with this person?

- Was she able to capture and summarise accurately what you were conveying to her?

- How challenged and excited did you feel – did you sense that the coach encouraged you to think differently or to make new connections?

- At the end, did you feel curious and stimulated to continue?

Testing the Coach's Approach and Quality

If you are satisfied with the answers to the above questions and feel that you have a sound intuitive basis for working with this coach, you then need to ascertain what else you need to know in order to make the decision about whether this coach offers you what you are looking for.

In particular, the importance of professional rigour and of supervision is emphasised in a report by the Institute of Employment Studies in the UK, published in 2001. This report surveyed a number of management development specialists and other commissioners/sponsors of coaching within companies and recommended that buyers of coaching services:

> enquire into the backgrounds, professional training and supervision arrangements of potential coaches to reassure themselves of the likely approach and concern for ongoing quality assurance that executive coaches have. (Carter, 2001)[5]

These are some questions that we recommend you ask any potential coach:

- *How do you work?*
  Listen particularly for a balance between structure and rigour with flexibility to tailor the approach to your unique needs

- *Based on my description of my situation and challenges, how do you feel you can support my development?*
  A competent and experienced coach will indicate where he or she feels able to provide the required development, and acknowledge where he or she may not

- *Can you give me any examples of when you have worked with similar clients/situations? How did they benefit?*

- *What was your training?*

- *What are your supervision arrangements?*

- *On what basis do you charge?*

Table 15.1 includes what we regard to be some good and bad signals from a coach.

If you are dealing with a coach working within an organisation, look for statements of mission, values and procedures. Check how open the coach

Table 15.1 Good and bad signals from a coach	
Good signs	**Bad signs**
■ Apparent interest in your story ■ Apparent energy/enthusiasm for working with you ■ Apparent 'comfort in his or her own skin' ■ Clarity about his or her philosophy and approach to coaching ■ A commitment to adding value and being held accountable for doing so ■ An appreciation for balancing the need for organisational and personal benefit from the process ■ A 'supportively challenging' presence	■ Talking too much ■ Telling too many 'war stories' (a sign of playing into a 'guru' role) ■ Seeming anxious to impress or ingratiating ■ Seeming in awe of you or your position ■ Sounding too formulaic ■ Feeling too directive ■ Encouraging a 'collusive' environment (where you are 'right' and others are 'wrong') ■ Letting you talk for too long without providing (gentle) focus on goals or structure for discussion ■ Operating in one style (for example all questions or all reflections) ■ Not picking up on your cues

or coaching concern is with regard to its procedures and its charges. Check the rigour of contracting and ask how progress is reported and measured. Check what the coach and the organisation do to support and invest in their own development.

Like most things in life, you are likely to get what you pay for. Therefore, unless you are severely restricted by budget, we recommend that you place price fairly low on your list of selection criteria. If all your other requirements are met, you are very likely to get a substantial return on your investment – both personally and organisationally.

Conclusion

As we described earlier in this chapter, and have argued throughout the book, we believe that professional coaching for leadership development has a substantial contribution to make to business and, in particular, to the leaders running businesses. Through providing a partnership of equals, development coaches can support leaders in addressing the challenges they face. Development coaching can assist leaders to learn by standing back from their context; it can help them develop leadership competence for that context; and, finally, it can help them to achieve balance in their often imbalanced lives.

However, with such an opportunity for professional coaches also comes a significant responsibility – both to clients and to their sponsoring organisations. We observe the coaching market to be expanding very rapidly, and feel that it is in the interest of all coaching professionals to conduct themselves with the highest standards and values. Equally, it is in the interest of all consumers and buyers of coaching services to be educated and sophisticated in their purchase of such services.

If we have any concern about the future of coaching, it lies in the common risk for all expanding markets – to grow without compromising on quality. We have tried to outline in this book the issues that both prospective clients and professional coaches should consider in their collaboration and hope that our input will at least contribute to the debate which is essential to the health of this important emerging discipline.

Notes

1. G. Hamel, 'Strategy Innovation and the Quest for Value', *Sloan Management Review*, Winter 1998, p. 7.
2. S. Ghoshal and C.A. Bartlett, *The Individualised Corporation: Great Companies Are Defined By Purpose, Process, and People* (London: Heinemann, 1998) pp. 313, 318.
3. J.E. Garten, *The Mind of the CEO* (Perseus, 2001).
4. F. Czerniawska, *Management Consultancy in the 21st Century* (London: Macmillan Business – now Palgrave, 1999) pp. 14, 35.
5. A. Carter, *Executive Coaching: Inspiring Performance at Work* (Insitute of Employment Studies, 2001) p. 38.

A Map of the Coaching Terrain

With such an explosion in coaching activity over the past five years, it has become difficult to discern the nature of this diverse activity, how it is being practised and what it is trying to achieve. We wish to attain greater clarity by mapping what we observe to be three key dimensions of the coaching activity occurring today:

1. Internally or externally delivered

2. Team or individual focused

3. Individually or corporately sponsored

With each dimension, we describe in this Appendix primarily the area that is *not* focused upon in this book.

Internally or Externally Delivered

Coaching is an activity that can be practised by members of an organisation or by external providers. A study in 1998 by the US-based HR consultancy, PDI, surveyed the HR departments of 93 Global 1000 organisations.[1] Of the companies in the UK, France and Singapore, 65% reported using coaching, whilst in the US it was 93%; 73% of companies reported that they used internal resources and 65% reported using external professionals.

It is worth noting that studies of both internal and external coaching activity are likely to be significantly underestimated due to the decentralised manner in which coaching is currently sourced. Indeed, the authors of the PDI study, David Peterson and Mary Hicks, noted that not one person they interviewed was willing to estimate either the amount of coaching taking place or the amount of money being spent on coaching services within their companies. While many HR departments are increasingly attempting to co-ordinate its usage, a large number of individual executives seek their own coaches and fund them (if externally provided) from their own budgets, unreported. Nevertheless, it is clear that there is a substantial and growing amount of coaching activity going on using both internal and external resources.

Internally Delivered

There are four ways in which coaching can be delivered internally, without the use of external suppliers:

1. *Coaching by senior managers* (playing a more classical 'mentoring' role)

2. *Coaching by line managers* (as a part of their management responsibilities)

3. *Coaching by HR professionals* (as a confidential service, for personal and professional reasons)

4. *Peer coaching* (as a way of encouraging colleagues to collaborate and share skills)

Coaching by Senior Managers

There has been a great deal of debate about the definitions of 'coaching' vs. 'mentoring', terms which have both been used to describe internally and externally provided one-to-one development. Historically, with origins in the eponymous myth of Mentor and Talemachus, mentoring was based on the concept of apprenticeship. This mythical origin implied an older, more experienced 'mentor' providing guidance and advice to a younger, and less experienced, 'apprentice'. The use of the terms mentoring and coaching have become muddled regarding whether they are referring to an internal or external activity and whether they denote a 'senior/junior' or more equal relationship. Therefore, for the purpose of clarity, we are electing to refer to all of the following dimensions and types of development activity as variations of coaching, which we will define further.

Companies often pair senior, more experienced executives with junior, less experienced managers as a way of passing on knowledge and experience within the organisation. The more experienced 'coach' and the person being coached do not have a reporting line relationship and the coach's role often includes brokering or sponsoring of the coached individual's career development (for example providing introductions to widen the individual's network or recommending him or her for a new position). There is a varying degree of formalisation of the terms of such relationships, for example the way in which the pairing is done, how frequently the pairs are encouraged to meet and how long their relationship is expected to last.

Coaching by Line Managers

Of the 73% of internal coaching activity identified by the Peterson and Hicks study, 50% was by line managers (including by senior managers, as described above). A 'coaching style of management' has come to describe a more holistic approach to managing subordinates. Managers are increasingly encouraged to convert themselves into coaches, and growing numbers of US companies are replacing the title of 'manager' with 'coach'. The majority of books about coaching are aimed at managers within organisations, guiding them through the process of coaching their staff. These 'coach managers' are expected to contribute to their staff's development, for example by:

- Providing clear performance expectations and feedback

- Teaching technical and functional skills as part of 'on-the-job training'

- Providing opportunities for the individual to try new things and learn from experience

- Creating a context for the individual's professional development beyond the scope of his or her current role

Coaching by HR Professionals

Of the 73% of internal coaching activity identified by the Peterson and Hicks study, 45% was by HR professionals. As the perceived 'people experts' in organisations, many HR professionals are the first port of call for their colleagues who are experiencing difficulties in performing their roles. They might be approached to discuss delicate or confidential matters, which colleagues do not feel they can discuss with their bosses, or they might be invited to facilitate a team as a more objective or expert internal resource. In addition, increasing numbers of HR professionals regard supporting senior executives as part of their official role.

Peer Coaching

Of the 73% of internal coaching activity identified by the study mentioned above, 5% was conducted by peers. Peer or 'co-coaching' provides a relationship in which colleagues can contract formally or informally as 'learning partners' or 'buddies'. They can take turns sharing their knowledge, skills or experience with each other in the context of mutual personal development rather than purely in the service of a shared task or project.

Externally Delivered

External coaching refers to a professional consultancy service provided by an external supplier for a fee. External coaches are typically either sole traders or employees of service organisations offering coaching as the only service or one of a range of related services. Such a consultancy service is the focus of this book.

Team or Individual Focused

Many coaches work with whole teams, as well as with individual members of the teams. Indeed, individual and team development conducted in parallel can be very complementary. However, it may be useful to distinguish between 'team coaching' and 'team facilitation', depending upon who is regarded as the primary client and whether the intervention comprises primarily group- or individual-based work.

Team Focused

In *team facilitation*, the client is the team. The focus of the coaching agenda is upon the overall team performance and development, and most interventions are delivered with the entire team present (either at a one-off event or as part of an ongoing development programme). Individual coaching sessions may be held in addition to team sessions, but primarily with the purpose of airing team-related issues, which may then be brought back to the team meeting. A beneficial by-product of team facilitation may be the development of each member of the team.

Individual Focused

In *team coaching*, each individual member of the team is a separate coaching client. However, because membership of the team defines the context for the coaching, the focus of each individual's coaching agenda is more likely to be upon his or her performance and development within the team than it would be if the individual were receiving one-to-one coaching in a less defined context. In practice, individual coaching sessions may discuss team issues, but primarily with a view to developing the individual's awareness and performance. In this sense, the beneficial by-product of team coaching is the converse of that with team facilitation, that is, the individuals' collective enhanced performance and development may lead to greater team performance. Team coaching is most commonly used to support a project team tasked with a specific set of objectives (for example a taskforce leading a specific change initiative).

Individually or Corporately Sponsored

Individually Sponsored Coaching

The US, in particular, has seen a huge growth in personal or life coaching with many variants under this umbrella (for example spiritual coaching, financial coaching, career coaching). The US is a success-driven culture, and individuals are eager to employ coaches as 'personal cheerleaders' to support their ambitions. Frederic Hudson's *The Handbook of Coaching* provides an excellent overview of the landscape of this market.[2]

The main issue distinguishing individually and corporately sponsored coaching is who is the client and therefore who owns the agenda. When the individual pays for his or her own coaching, he or she is the only client and therefore in complete control of the agenda. According to a 1998 survey by the International Coach Federation, almost all clients in the US seeking personal coaching are professionals, with 82% having college degrees and an annual average income of $63,000. Of clients surveyed, 98.5% said their investment in a personal coach was worth the money. The most common reasons for seeking a personal coach were for help with:

- time management (81%)
- career guidance (74%)
- business advice (74%)

The top five benefits for most clients were:

- a higher level of self-awareness (68%)

- smarter goal setting (62%)

- a more balanced life (61%)

- reduced stress levels (57%)

- more self-confidence (52%)

As this research indicates, the agendas in individually sponsored personal coaching primarily concern career management issues. Even though these personal coaching clients spend most of their coaching time discussing work-related issues, the fact that they are paying for the coaching themselves means that the agenda can be focused entirely on their objectives in the service of furthering their careers.

Corporately Sponsored Coaching

When the organisation pays for the coaching, two clients are created and a balance must be achieved within the coaching agenda between corporate and individual goals. This book is about corporately sponsored coaching and explores this required balance in much greater detail.

Notes

1. D.B. Peterson and M.D. Hicks, 'Professional Coaching: State of the Art, State of the Practice'. Keynote address at The Art and Practice of Coaching Leaders, sponsored by the University of Maryland's National Leadership Institute and Personnel Decisions International, Washington, DC, October 1998.
2. F.M. Hudson, The Handbook of Coaching (San Francisco: Jossey-Bass, 1999).

Three Schools of Psychology and Counselling

There are three main schools of Western psychology – psychoanalytic, cognitive–behavioural and humanistic. Whether implicitly or explicitly, development coaches practise primarily from one of these orientations.

Since each school is based upon a different philosophical perspective on the human condition, a coach's own orientation is likely to have a profound impact on how he or she practises. While we do not have space to present an exhaustive description of each, we have provided below a very brief description of each of the three schools and how they are likely to influence a coach practising from that orientation.

A Psychodynamic Orientation

Freud is regarded as the originator of psychoanalysis. Since he developed his original theories (circa 1900), his ideas have been substantially modified and developed by other practitioners of psychoanalysis, many of whom now describe their practice as psychodynamic. Therapists and coaches working in the Freudian tradition tend to make similar kinds of assumptions about the nature of the client's issues, and the manner in which these issues can best be addressed. According to John McLeod, the main distinctive features of the psychodynamic approach are:

- An assumption that the client's difficulties have their ultimate origins in childhood experiences

- An assumption that the client may not be consciously aware of the true motives or impulses behind his or her actions
- The use in counselling and therapy of techniques such as dream analysis and interpretation of the transference relationship[1]

Although coaches do not work therapeutically with clients in the way described in the last point, they will tend to operate based on the first two assumptions McLeod describes. This typically manifests itself in the coaching process in two ways:

1. The coach will start by taking a detailed life history, including a description of early family life and influences

2. The coach will encourage the client to connect difficulties he or she may be experiencing today in his or her work life with their possible origins in early life

Richard Kilburg openly declares his own psychodynamic orientation in his book *Executive Coaching: Developing Managerial Wisdom in a World of Chaos*. In a case study, he illustrates the influence of this orientation well:

> In one very productive coaching session, Ann was able to connect the pattern of conflict at work with the history of interpersonal and emotional trouble she experienced in her family of origin.[2]

Kilburg explains what he sees as the relevance of the psychodynamic model to coaching:

> The inner world of the person is organized into complex and varied patterns that are expressed in and through the different social relationships engaged in during an average day. Consultants and coaches are primarily concerned with people in their roles and relationships at work, yet we see in the elements of the [psychodynamic] model that the inner experience of any one of the individuals whom we try to help is characterized by a rich landscape of structures and processes. Awareness of conflicts, defences, and the emotional and cognitive elements of human experience is vital for consultants and coaches, because the origins of most forms of resistance to change can be found in the internal interaction of these elements of the model.[3]

Finally, he spells out the implications for coaches' own training and development:

I firmly believe that consultants must have at least a rudimentary understanding of the nature and extent to which unconscious forces shape behavior for individuals, groups and organizations. I also believe that consultants must be able to manage their own emotional and psychodynamic responses to clients and change initiatives and to assist their client in doing the same ... The ability to weave the knowledge and skills of psychodynamic and emotional management into the ongoing challenges and tasks of leading, managing and changing organizational systems greatly adds to the likelihood that any consultation project will succeed.[4]

A Cognitive–Behavioural Orientation

The behavioural dimension of the cognitive–behavioural school has its origins in behavioural psychology, which was created in the early 20th century by the American, J.B. Watson (based upon earlier work by Pavlov and Skinner). Behavioural psychology is based upon the belief that human beings are conditioned by their experiences and that their behaviour can therefore be 'reprogrammed' by exposing them to new experiences.

In the 1960s, the former psychoanalysts Aaron Beck and Albert Ellis were influential in introducing a cognitive dimension to the behavioural approach, particularly through attention to dysfunctional thought processes and irrational beliefs.

McLeod describes three key features of cognitive behaviourism:

- A problem-solving, change-focused approach to working with clients
- A respect for scientific values
- Close attention to the cognitive processes through which people monitor and control their behaviour[5]

As David Statt states:

where a psychoanalyst would regard neurotic behaviour as being simply a symptom and direct his efforts at finding the underlying causes of that symptom, the behaviourist believes that there are no underlying causes; the 'symptom' is all there is, and that is what needs to be changed.[6]

Statt speculates on why this approach found particularly widespread interest in the American business world:

> The effect of Behaviourism on American life was to go far beyond psychology or the academic sphere. In its clearly stated, no-nonsense style concentrating on an objective and apparently common sense view of the human condition, it seems to me reminiscent of the recently introduced principles of Taylorism in the world of work. Both 'isms' seemed to have a similar appeal for many people in early twentieth century American society, with its roaring economy and the sense of endless opportunity that attracted millions of immigrants from all over the world. Behaviourism was part of a simple 'can-do' philosophy for a time and place that was growing impatient with its European heritage. It was a vigorous antidote to Social Darwinism and its denial of environmental influences. It was an affirmation of the fundamental American belief that people could better themselves by their own efforts.[7]

Indeed, cognitive–behavioural therapy is very pragmatic and thus lends itself well to coaching. McLeod provides a description of a typical cognitive–behavioural approach to therapy, which may be loosely translated into the coaching process as follows:

1. Establishing rapport and creating a working alliance between coach and client

2. Assessing the client's strengths and limitations

3. Setting goals or targets for change. These should be selected by the client, and be clear, specific and attainable

4. Applying coaching skills and techniques (cognitive–behaviourally based coaching techniques might include having the client keep a journal to raise awareness of his or her thoughts and feelings in response to certain situations, situation analysis and problem solving, action planning to experiment with different ways of behaving, post-mortem analysis of specific events)

5. Monitoring progress

6. Ending and evaluating results against the goals established at the beginning of the coaching contract

A Humanistic Orientation

The emergence of client- or person-centred therapy in the 1950s was part of a movement in American psychology to create an alternative to the two theories which dominated the field at that time: psychoanalysis and behaviourism. According to McLeod:

> This movement became known as the 'third force' ... as humanistic psychology ... a vision of a psychology that would have a place for the human capacity for creativity, growth and choice, influenced by the European tradition of existential and phenomenological philosophy. The image of the person in humanistic psychology is of a self striving to find meaning and fulfilment in the world. Humanistic psychology has always consisted of a broad set of theories and models connected by shared values and philosophical assumptions ... the most widely used humanistic approaches are person-centred and Gestalt, although psychosynthesis, transactional analysis and other models also contain strong humanistic elements. The common ingredient in all humanistic approaches is an emphasis on experiential processes. Rather than focusing on the origins of client problems in childhood events (psychodynamic) or the achievement of new patterns of behaviour in the future (behavioural), humanistic therapies concentrate on the 'here-and-now' experiencing of the client.[8]

Statt provides further insight into the distinctions between the three approaches:

> Carl Rogers is often taken to be the primary personality theorist in humanistic psychology, which 'opposes what it regards as the bleak pessimism and despair inherent in the psychoanalytic view of humans on the one hand, and the robot conception of humans portrayed in Behaviourism on the other hand.' Humanistic psychology takes an optimistic view of the existence of creativity and potential for growth within every human being ... Freud's underlying view of human nature was that people are driven largely by irrational forces which only a well-ordered society can hold in check. Rogers on the other hand believed that people are basically rational and are motivated to fulfil themselves and become the best human beings that they can be.[9]

Notes

1. J. McLeod, *An Introduction to Counselling*, 2nd edn (Buckingham: Open University Press, 1999) p. 33.

2. R. Kilburg, *Executive Coaching: Developing Managerial Wisdom in a World of Chaos* (Washington, DC: American Psychological Association, 2000) p. 5.
3. Ibid., p. 38.
4. Ibid., pp. 16–17.
5. J. McLeod, *An Introduction to Counselling*, 2nd edn (Buckingham: Open University Press, 1999) p. 62.
6. D.A. Statt, *Psychology and the World of Work* (London: Macmillan – now Palgrave, 1994) p. 175.
7. Ibid., p. 19.
8. J. McLeod, *An Introduction to Counselling*, 2nd edn (Buckingham: Open University Press, 1999) pp. 88–9.
9. D.A. Statt, *Psychology and the World of Work* (London: Macmillan – now Palgrave, 1994) p. 177.

INDEX